Classroom Management

Class room

MANAGEMENT

Strategies for Achievement, Cooperation + Engagement

NANCY STEINEKE

HEINEMANN
Portsmouth, NH

Heinemann
361 Hanover Street
Portsmouth, NH 03801–3912
www.heinemann.com

Offices and agents throughout the world

The author and publisher wish to thank those who have generously given permission to reprint borrowed material:

Figure 1.2: "Figure 4: Factors Teachers Report as Being Very Important for Leaving Teaching" from *Teacher Turnover: Why It Matters and What We Can Do About It* by Desiree Carver-Thomas and Linda Darling-Hammond. Copyright © 2017. Published by the Learning Policy Institute, Palo Alto, CA. Reprinted by permission of the Publisher.

Acknowledgments for borrowed material continue on page 227.

Library of Congress Cataloging-in-Publication Data
Names: Steineke, Nancy, author.
Title: Classroom management : strategies for achievement, cooperation, and engagement / Nancy Steineke.
Description: Portsmouth, NH : Heinemann, 2020. | Includes bibliographical references.
Identifiers: LCCN 2019055940 | ISBN 9780325109534
Subjects: LCSH: Classroom management.
Classification: LCC LB3013 .S6594 2020 | DDC 371.102/4—dc23
LC record available at https://lccn.loc.gov/2019055940

Editor: Tobey Antao
Editorial coordinator: Catrina Marshall
Production: Vicki Kasabian
Copy editor: Jennifer Brett Greenstein
Cover design: Suzanne Heiser
Text design: Monica A. Crigler
Typesetter: Kim Arney
Manufacturing: Steve Bernier

Printed in the United States of American on acid-free paper
1 2 3 4 5 6 7 8 9 10   CGB   25 24 23 22 21 20
March 2020 Printing

CONTENTS

Online Resources, noted throughout this book, can be found on Heinemann's product page for *Classroom Management*:

http://hein.pub/classman

ACKNOWLEDGMENTS

Writing a book is a crabby, cranky business. A big thanks goes to my husband, Bill Steineke, for continuing to patiently hold my hand.

Believe it or not, it takes quite a few talented people to move a book from an idea kernel to actual publication. I am indebted to my incredible Heinemann team (they're all listed toward the bottom of page iv, so take a look!) for making my book a tangible reality. And since I know they will already be fully immersed in their next publishing project when this book hits the presses, I will leave them with the words of Douglas Adams, author of *The Hitchhiker's Guide to the Galaxy*: "So long, and thanks for all the fish."

* * *

These classroom management moves are the culmination of my own work with students over thirty-seven years as well as my continued work with teachers across the country. I would like to give a special thanks to those classroom teachers in grades 4–12 who generously shared their time, thinking, and classroom photos with me:

Lauren Allinder, seventh grade, Hernando Middle School, Hernando, Mississippi; Andrea Arndt, seventh grade, Southaven Middle School, Southaven, Mississippi; Anna (Dunlap) Chapman, fourth grade, Macon Hall Elementary, Cordova, Tennessee; Brittany Elliott, sixth grade, Alvin Middle School, Alvin, Texas; David Finkle, ninth grade, Deland High School, Deland, Florida; Sheila Furey Sullivan, grades 9–12, Andrew High School, Tinley Park, Illinois; Carol Gallegos, curriculum specialist, Hanford Elementary SD, Hanford, California; Anjali Williams, sixth grade, Woodrow Wilson Middle School, Hanford, California; Mayra Martin, sixth grade, Woodrow Wilson Middle School, Hanford, California; Colleen Ghelfi, grades 9–12, Andrew High School, Tinley Park, Illinois; Melissa Hoeft, fifth grade, Gray M. Sanborn Elementary, Palatine, Illinois; Lauren Huddleston, seventh grade, Hutchison School, Memphis, Tennessee; Monifa Johnson, assistant principal, DeSoto Central High School, DeSoto, Mississippi; Lindsey Jones, seventh grade, Hernando Middle School, Hernando, Mississippi;

Lauren Allinder

Andrea Arndt

Anna (Dunlap) Chapman

Brittany Elliott

David Finkle

Sheila Furey Sullivan

Carol Gallegos, Anjali Williams, Mayra Martin

Colleen Ghelfi

Melissa Hoeft

Lauren Huddleston

Monifa Johnson

Lindsey Jones

Cindi Koudelka

Mitch Lazarus

Jenna Leser

Laura Olson

Dan Weinstein

THANK YOU!

Cindi Koudelka, eighth grade, Fieldcrest Middle School, Wenona, Illinois; Mitch Lazarus, grades 4–8, formerly of Chicago Public Schools, now leading mindfulness classes for teens and adults; Jenna Leser, fifth grade, St. Margaret of Scotland, Chicago, Illinois; Laura Olson, fourth grade, Eason Elementary School, Waukee, Iowa; and Dan Weinstein, twelfth grade, Great Neck South High School, Long Island, New York.

My attic office would be a lonely place if it weren't for my personal assistant cat, LizLemon. Unfortunately, Double L took far more interest in my initial drafting than she did in my revision work. I guess she hasn't read Barry Lane's *After The End*.

LizLemon

1

Reducing the Stress of Classroom Management

I don't know about you, but my first year of teaching was not pretty. At the time, I was teaching home economics: a semester-long senior class called Food Service and several sections of Freshman Survey. Oh, and did I mention that I was twenty-one years old? I guess that made me old enough looking to the freshmen, but I was only three or four (or sometimes two) years older than the seniors. I'm sure I reminded them of an older sister bossing them around. One girl, in particular, really had it out for me. She was very angry. And I had no idea what to do about it.

I had no guidance. My colleagues advised me not to smile until Christmas. My preservice methods instructors told me that classroom discipline is very personal and develops over time. Neither piece of advice was at all useful. With an empty toolkit, I responded to this angry girl the only way I knew—by mirroring her anger. After all, that was what all my teachers in high school had done. I yelled and I punished. Although I got her to comply more often, our conflict simmered for the entire semester. Neither of us was sad to say good-bye to the other on the last day of class.

Thankfully, the second-semester senior class went more smoothly. Not because I had learned anything, but because they were just more compliant. Even though the rough classroom waters had calmed a bit, I still remember marking a big *X* on each calendar square until I finally reached summer vacation.

I wish I could say it's rare for new teachers to be frustrated by classroom management, but it's not. I've heard stories from teachers from around the country about how classroom management loomed large in their early years of teaching. Here are a few that have stayed with me:

- Fifth-grade teacher Melissa Hoeft walked in to her first year of teaching with a "tough love" vision. She found that being tough worked for about a third of her students, but the other two-thirds remained unmoved by her "logical consequences" and inflexible compliance expectations. The following year she tried using tangible rewards: classroom currency. Exhibit the correct behavior and eventually you can use your currency to purchase a trip to the treasure box or a get-out-of-homework pass. As Alfie Kohn (2018) would have predicted, students were not internalizing positive class behavior and, instead, kept "charging more" for maintaining the behaviors necessary for the class to run smoothly. Tired of the inflation and the record keeping a currency system requires, Melissa moved on to a clip chart, with equally dismal results. She observed a few students thriving on the public and competitive aspect of teacher pleasing while the bulk of her students failed to improve their self-regulation while enduring daily public humiliation. But it was the clip chart that provided her epiphany: What if there were a clip chart for teachers in the main hallway and the principal clipped everyone up or down during the course of the day for everyone to ogle as they walked out of school at the end of the day?

- Monifa Johnson turned out to be a natural when it came to showing her high school students who the boss was. Her students were so quiet and compliant that the principal who was observing her teaching paid her what he thought was the ultimate compliment: smiling, he declared, "You sure do have your foot on the throat of every one of your students!" Monifa's evaluation was glowing, particularly the section on classroom management, but the observation left her feeling hollow as she wondered how she had become a disciplinarian rather than a teacher.

Perhaps pieces of these stories sound familiar to you? In my experience, and in the experience of teachers at every grade level with whom I've worked, discussions of classroom management are often tinged with frustration, anger, and fear. Teachers—people who got into this field because they legitimately like kids—soon feel that their jobs are to "control" students, to be the voice of order in the midst of chaos. Before we know what's happened, we find ourselves trapped in a rigid discipline system, trying to keep order, while our hopes for a joyful and engaging course fall by the wayside. There's often also a disturbing feeling that classroom management is somehow out of one's hands, that it's up to the luck of the class roster to determine whether your class will be "good" or "bad." That comment about how classroom management develops over time turned out to be true for me, for Melissa, for Monifa, and for many more of us, too. After many mistakes and some extensive cooperative learning training with David W. Johnson, Roger T. Johnson, and Edythe Holubec (2008) my classes were orderly, engaged, and even happy. Melissa dumped the clip chart and concluded that the best and only way to "manage" a class is by knowing students, listening to students, and believing in students unconditionally. Monifa resolved to recalibrate her classroom from a traditional approach to a collaborative approach.

I'm proud of the decades I spent in the classroom, of the shifts that I made to manage my classroom more effectively, of the successes I had with students, and of the success they found at school as a result of our well-run, collaborative classroom. However, it was certainly a disservice to my students and to me that my classroom management refinement was a result of trial and error paired with a summer district institute that I had fortuitously signed up for.

The problem of leaving teachers to try to figure out classroom management through trial and error has powerful and far-reaching effects. For starters, students who have suffered through years of ill-managed classrooms or who have borne the brunt of an authoritarian teacher are much less likely to see school as a meaningful place for them, which curtails their learning and their future options. In addition, the pernicious school-to-prison pipeline, which *Teaching Tolerance* magazine describes as "discipline policies that push students out of the classroom and into the criminal justice system at alarming rates," thrives when classroom management is ineffective, especially in "zero tolerance" schools (Elias 2013). Finally, the job dissatisfaction that results from constant struggles for order contributes to the high rates of teacher attrition that currently plague our field and prevents schools from building teams of veteran teachers.

What Doesn't Work: The Traditional Approach to Classroom Management

I'm not proud of my attempts at classroom management during my first year of teaching, but I came by them honestly: they're the methods that I saw at work as a student every day from first through twelfth grade. And, while each new grade (or, in secondary school, each new course) brought a new teacher, my classmates and I found that the expectations did not change: our primary job at school was compliance, not learning.

Throughout elementary and middle school my teachers focused on teaching us the consequences of misbehavior using various demerit systems. One free warning and then your name went up on the humiliation board. Depending on how many demerits you got in a day, the consequences varied from losing recess to receiving an after-school detention to attending a mandatory conference with your parents or guardians in tow. Thanks to those demerit systems, I spent most of my elementary school days being quiet, fearful, and nervous with my stomach tied in knots.

If you are a student of more recent vintage, demerits might not ring a bell, but their progeny live on in the form of clip charts. With name-labeled clothespins at the ready, teachers publicly identify who is a "super student" or "role model." At the beginning of each day, all the clips roost at "ready to learn," but they then scurry up the positive scale or depressingly descend to lower, vaguely threatening levels of "better think about it" or "make better choices." A student's clip hits rock bottom in the square red rectangle of "call home." And remember, this chart offers each student a daily opportunity for public recognition or public shaming. I shudder to think about the messages these behavior management techniques etch into the psyche of students (Jung and Smith 2018).

In high school, teachers traded in the demerit systems for group punishment. Playing the innocent bystander part in a very unruly sophomore English class, I remember our young first-year teacher (taking the advice of a more experienced veteran) running a stopwatch every time the class veered off task. Then, as the passing bell rang, she announced triumphantly that we were all going to sit there in our seats for the exact amount of time we had wasted. As you might have guessed, the compliant majority silently gritted their teeth, took it, and resolved to hate this teacher forever because we would be late for our next class and receive an undeserved tardy. But, as you might have guessed, the unruly minority bellowed in outrage and told the teacher where she could put her stopwatch. These kids had spent grades 1–8 with their names written in permanent marker on the demerit list. They had "clipped down" so many times that their clothespins were permanently red. The opportunity to vent their frustrations of so many years was totally worth one more trip to the dean's office, another referral added to the file. Our teacher's attempt at controlling us failed miserably and, in fact, escalated the conflict, firmly pitting the entire class against her. She resigned a few weeks later.

Now you might be thinking, "No wonder that didn't work; it's so punitive! Your teachers should have used rewards and positive reinforcement." Unfortunately, rewards have the same goal as punishment: compliance, not learning. Additionally, rewards do little to change long-term behavior. Adolescent brains, in particular, are wired for impulsivity and are far less receptive to rewards than those of either younger children or adults (Armstrong 2016). If an adolescent is given the choice between receiving a relatively worthless candy bar two days from now or blurting out the perfect wisecrack right now, the wisecrack is going to win. In addition, significant research has proven that offering students (or any humans) extrinsic rewards actually makes them *less* interested and invested in a given task. After all, if the behavior is worth doing, why would you need an extrinsic reward to get you to do it? (Alfie Kohn's brilliant *Punished by Rewards* [2018] explores this topic in more depth.)

Though a system of numerous sticks with possibly a few carrots (the most common carrot being "Behave and I, the teacher, will leave you alone"), might induce student compliance in the moment, it does damage in the long run. Our students might learn to be quiet and follow our directions without question, but do these students' behaviors prepare them to be independent learners beyond your classroom? Do they reflect deep content learning? No. They simply teach students how to survive your class. While I easily remembered and told my stories of compliance-based schooling just now, I have no equally vivid memories of deep learning. How sad for me and my teachers. And here's what's worse: while it's been quite some time since I was a student, my work in a wide variety of today's schools has shown me that the focus on compliance is just as strong now as it was back then.

What Works: A Collaborative Approach

Take a moment to think of a class in which you were a student or a visitor and in which the students were focused, productive, and (this last one is crucial) *content*. Now, try to remember what you noticed about the teacher's classroom management on a typical day. Did the teacher spend a lot of time enumerating rules and policing the classroom? Did the teacher threaten the students with punishment for misbehavior or offer rewards for compliance? Probably not, right?

In a classroom in which the kids are focused, productive, and content (or even *happy*), you might be hard-pressed to name specific things that the teacher does regarding classroom management during a typical day. It might even seem as though the teacher didn't do *anything* related to classroom management and that the kids were simply "good" all on their own. But, in my experience, I've yet to see a classroom like this come together all on its own. Building this kind of learning environment requires a long-term commitment from the teacher, with a clear focus on collaborating with students rather than demanding compliance from students.

One of the first mistakes we often make as teachers is that we assume that we and the students are on different teams. We are all Marshal Will Kane in *High Noon*, abandoned by the rest of the town and left to face a ruthless band of outlaws alone. It is our job to *take control*, to *make them pay attention*. When we begin the year—or even the school day—with the idea that it is our job to control and contain students, our job immediately becomes less joyful, less sustainable, and less possible to do effectively. Think about it: Can you imagine a situation in which you could be focused, productive, and happy while someone was actively and continually trying to micromanage you? I doubt it. And yet, we expect our students to do just that, from the time they are old enough to learn to read and write until they are legally adults. We may even have felt that something was deeply wrong with this situation: If we became educators because we care about kids, why are we so often at odds with them? If school is a place to learn and grow, why do we spend so much time correcting and disciplining?

If we want students to be active learners, participants, and citizens in our classrooms, we can't spend our days together ordering them around and asserting, in large and small ways, that we are the alpha dogs. Instead of working in opposition with our students, we can take a more productive approach by deciding to manage the classroom *with* our students, collaborating with them to build a classroom community. Let's take another look at that classroom you recalled earlier: Did the teacher seem to have a good relationship with the students? Did the students seem to have good relationships with one another? Did the students seem to understand the classroom expectations? Did the students seem interested in their work? They did, didn't they? That's because the teacher established a *community*, not a classroom based on rules and consequences. The reason we didn't see evidence of the teacher forcing the kids to comply in this classroom is that there was no need for it: the kids had made the *choice* to be productive members of the classroom, so they didn't need coercion.

Expanding responsibility to your students in a thoughtful and scaffolded way isn't losing control: it is freeing for everyone. Imagine how different and more rewarding your role as a teacher is when you do not have to be the center of all authority, wisdom, knowledge, planning, and answers. If a problem arises, it is the class' responsibility to help create a solution, not just yours. You will find that nurturing a classroom community of invested learners energizes you and your students because it is less stressful for everyone.

But a collaborative approach does more than provide an orderly class period for you and your students: it also has truly incredible long-term results.

A collaborative approach promotes academic achievement.

Students who work together effectively show higher academic achievement than students who work competitively or on their own (Johnson and Johnson 2018):

> *[S]tudents working cooperatively tended to be more involved in activities and tasks, attach greater importance to success, and engage in more on-task behavior and less apathetic, off-task, disruptive behaviors. . . . [C]ooperative experiences, compared with competitive and individualistic ones, have been found to promote more positive attitudes toward the task and the experience of working on the task. (co-operation.org/what-is-cooperative-learning)*

A collaborative approach develops interpersonal skills.

By involving students in managing the class, building community, and working through rough spots, we model how to acknowledge issues and work together in a positive manner that engages the expertise of all parties while eliminating the screaming, arguing, or anger that can otherwise creep into classroom conflicts. Research bears out the importance of collaboration in building these interpersonal skills: The more students collaborate, the better they are able to take other people's perspectives into account when making decisions (Johnson 2009). Furthermore, as students practice these skills in the context of academic collaboration, they internalize and refine these skills (McGinnis 2012).

A collaborative approach bolsters social and emotional learning.

Managing your classroom *with* your students strengthens the five core competencies of social and emotional learning (as defined by CASEL, the Collaborative for Academic, Social, and Emotional Learning): self-awareness, self-management, social awareness, relationship skills, and responsible decision-making (https://casel.org/what-is-sel/). The benefits of social and emotional learning are well documented. In a meta-analysis of 213 experimentally controlled studies of K–12 students who participated in social–emotional learning, students showed an 11 percent average gain in academic performance when compared with those who received no explicit social–emotional instruction. Additionally, teachers reported fewer episodes of disruption, aggression, or bullying. The study also includes a finding of great importance to us classroom teachers: the effects of social–emotional learning were strongest when teachers infused these lessons into their content and students practiced these behaviors in the context of working together as they studied the content (Durlak et al. 2011).

A collaborative approach supports students' empathy and happiness.

In case you still doubt the necessity of creating a caring, kind, collaborative community, this research from Harvard is worth considering. In 2014, the Harvard Graduate School of Education released a report called the *Making Caring Common Project*. Early on in the report are some statistics that you might find startling and—quite frankly— troubling. Surveying over 10,000 middle and high school students in 33 schools that reflected diverse geographic, socioeconomic, and ethnic representation, researchers asked students to rank what was most important to them: achieving at a high level, happiness, or caring for others. While almost 80 percent of the students surveyed made happiness or achievement their top choice, only 20 percent chose caring for others.

Students also ranked fairness low in relation to several other values. For example, they were far more likely to rank "hard work" above fairness. Some students made it quite clear to the researchers that their self-interest is paramount: "If you are not happy, life is nothing. After that, you want to do well. And after that, expend any excess energy on others."

The irony of all this self-absorption is that it doesn't really help anyone in the long run. The report goes on to assert that students exclusively focused on personal achievement and happiness are both less caring of others and *less* happy. Plus, when caring for others is not a priority, students are less likely to exhibit empathy. And without the ability to empathize, students are much more likely to bully, a phenomenon of particular importance in middle school and high school because a recent study by the National Research Council found that students used strategic, calculated bullying in order to establish social dominance (Willard 2017). Although bullying might offer the bully some immediate satisfaction, engaging in such behavior is troubling, because child bullies grow into adults who have little concern for the welfare of others.

> *Any healthy society depends on adults who are able to take responsibility for diverse members of their communities and to put, at pivotal times, the common good before their own. Our research suggests that we are not preparing children to create this kind of society.*

The Harvard study concluded that our students "need ongoing opportunities to practice caring and helpfulness, sometimes with guidance from adults" (Making Caring Common Project 2014). Guess what? *We* are the adult guidance that report was referring to! When collaborative values permeate our classroom, students will rise to the challenge and achieve their potentials; that same study bears that out as well. Furthermore, combining the explicit teaching of social skills and the explicit teaching of multiple perspective taking results in even greater empathy and positive behavior toward classmates (Grizenko et al. 2000).

A collaborative approach aligns with brain development.

By fourth grade, children begin to see the world in terms of fairness and justice, so it's unsurprising that we see students pushing back on a teacher's actions if they consider those actions to be are unfair, coercive, or just not their idea. This gradual brain maturation is the reason why elementary school students may begin to display tempers and physical outbursts as they approach the age of ten (Wood 2007). In middle school and high school, traditional compliance-based approaches to classroom management often fail spectacularly because they ignore adolescents' needs for connection, safety, and independence. Across all these grade levels, the most effective, humane, and brain-compatible classroom management approach is collaborative.

A collaborative approach gives students a feeling of safety.

Feeling protected and connected is what enables children, adolescents, and adults to do their best learning (Cozolino 2013). When humans are under stress, their ability to learn and to retrieve memories suffers (Vogel and Schwabe 2016). This need for safety becomes even more critical for adolescents as their accelerated emotional development makes them more vulnerable to stress than elementary-aged children or adults are. The limbic system, the part of the brain that responds with emotion, starts developing at a faster rate than the prefrontal cortex, the part of the brain responsible for executive functioning such as decision-making, planning, inhibiting impulses, and self-control (Armstrong 2016). This often causes students to react to stress with anger, anxiety, distress, or depression—none of which are conducive to learning (Hammond 2014). Using management techniques that shame or embarrass can quickly shut down learning for students of any age, but they construct a powerful recipe for failure for our older students: not only do negative emotions "in the moment" prevent learning, but negative past experiences influence and shape attitudes toward future learning as well (Posey 2019). As a matter of fact, research has highlighted the connection between shaming and later delinquency (Braithwaite 1989). A collaborative classroom management approach includes creating a low-stress environment, one in which each student feels welcomed, supported, and valued (see Figure 1.1) (Cozolino 2013; Hammond 2014).

A collaborative approach gives students a feeling of belonging.

Peer inclusion is of paramount importance to students, and being excluded creates more severe distress for adolescents than for adults (Armstrong 2016). When older students feel they are disliked in a class, their ability to learn is inhibited, resulting in academic loss of about half a year (Hattie 2009). A collaborative classroom managements approach is intentional, providing students multiple opportunities for positive interactions with

Figure 1.1 **When students feel safe, they can take risks and give 110 percent, which might mean jumping up on a chair in order to enhance their performance!**

peers. An added bonus is that the more students talk about content, building upon and expanding upon one another's ideas, the better they learn (Moore, Michael, and Penick-Parks 2018).

A collaborative approach promotes executive functioning.

When students are included in problem-solving and decision-making, they become more accustomed to thinking flexibly. When students use reflection, self-assessment, and mindfulness, their stress decreases and their self-control and regulation increase. As students work together in meaningful and productive ways, they develop greater capacity for perspective taking and empathy (Medina 2018).

Also, how we design group work for students needs to be intentional. We often expect students to arrive in our classroom already knowing how to work with others effectively, yet our students may never have had direct instruction in the social skills necessary to do so. We must teach, practice, and refine our students' prosocial behaviors explicitly since they are the foundation for developing positive relationships (Frey, Fisher, and Smith 2019). As students gain social and emotional skills, they increase their ability to set goals, make decisions, solve conflicts and interpersonal problems, and get along while reducing disruptive behavior.

Something else about adolescent brains in particular: they behave inconsistently. When a situation is emotionally charged, an adolescent's emotions are more likely to overtake their reasoning (Armstrong 2016), preventing them from fully understanding the power of their words and actions. As adults with fully developed prefrontal cortexes and well-established executive function, we might be offended, horrified, or disgusted by what is said in the heat of the moment by a student. And, very possibly, someday the student who spoke those words will reflect on the incident and see it differently than they did at the time. In the meantime, a collaborative approach can support students' understanding of their own emotions and can help them make better choices when speaking and acting (Moore, Michael, and Penick-Parks 2018).

A collaborative approach makes strong teacher–student relationships possible.

The stronger the teacher–student relationship, the safer the student feels, thus lowering the student's stress while increasing learning and executive functioning. Strong relationships are built on mutual respect. While respect in school is often narrowly defined by adults as following the rules and avoiding disruptive behaviors, true respect comes when teachers deliberately build a bridge between their own perspectives and the realities of their students (Emdin 2016). In a collaborative classroom, teachers offer students respect by knowing them and really listening to what they have to say, recognizing that their interpretation of a student's behavior might be significantly different from the student's intentions. Collaboration enables us to study our students, building trust as we work to emphasize each student's power, skills, and gifts (Milner et al. 2018; Moore, Michael, and Penick-Parks 2018; Ladson-Billings 2009).

A collaborative approach is better for *you*.

It's hard to be the only marshal in town. The stress of feeling like the lone voice of order and righteousness in the classroom does not inspire great teaching. Additionally, we live in a time when people—both adults and our students—may write off empathy and caring as unnecessary. When we and our students are feeling the push of academic goals and assessments, it often happens that community, empathy, consideration, and kindness—while still lauded as admirable—get little real attention, especially in the years beyond primary school.

Yet establishing a caring classroom community is just as helpful to us as it is to our students. While at times it seems present-day society becomes more divided by the hour, continually fueling an "us or them" mentality, not one iota of that perspective will serve us well in the classroom. When you throw uncooperative student behavior issues onto the already mounting pile of teacher frustrations—high-stakes testing, unreasonable accountability expectations, and the need to do more with less—it's not surprising that teacher turnover is ever increasing. A 2017 research report published by the Learning Policy Institute (Carver-Thomas and Darling-Hammond) reveals that the number one reason teachers change schools or leave the profession completely is dissatisfaction (see Figure 1.2).

Of course, dissatisfaction encompasses many, many facets of the job. However, it is a guarantee that when we dwell in a negative classroom environment day in and day out, when we find ourselves policing students rather than teaching, we will feel burned-out and dissatisfied. Therefore, just for our own self-preservation and mental health maintenance, we must work with our students from day one to create safe, livable environments.

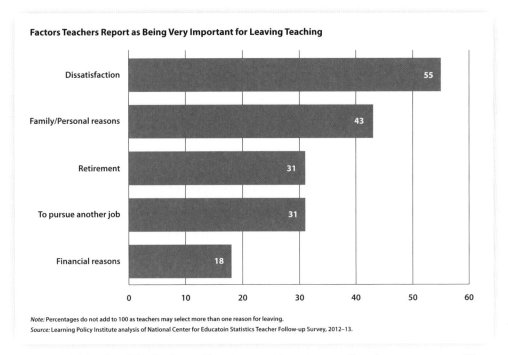

Factors Teachers Report as Being Very Important for Leaving Teaching

Note: Percentages do not add to 100 as teachers may select more than one reason for leaving.
Source: Learning Policy Institute analysis of National Center for Educatoin Statistics Teacher Follow-up Survey, 2012–13.

Figure 1.2 **Might dissatisfaction lower if teachers could create rewarding classroom communities where all felt safe, appreciated, and respected?**

How This Book Can Help

At this point, you might be wondering, "This all sounds good, but how do I make it happen?" The underlying principle of collaborative classroom management is *to involve the learner at every step*. This seemingly simple idea is the part of the recipe that is often missing from approaches we might consider more traditional, but it's at the heart of every suggestion in this book.

Collaborative classroom management doesn't happen in a vacuum. You need to actively build your classroom community starting before students even set foot in your classroom, with an especially strong push in the early days and weeks of school, and constant maintenance for the remainder of your time with the class. Don't worry, this isn't as time-consuming as it sounds, and it is much, much more pleasant and efficient than the alternative: continually playing disciplinary whack-a-mole with random issues as they pop up in a traditional classroom. If class problems are interfering with your students' focus and learning, then the problem is already wasting precious days because few are remembering your content. Students are also more willing to work with you and more willing to change behavior when you've built a supportive classroom community with them and involved them in any necessary problem-solving.

As you peruse the pages, you'll find that this book is organized sequentially and lays out a comprehensive plan for collaborative classroom management across a semester or school year. Each chapter offers a collection of teaching "moves"—specific, ready-to-use ideas and guidance for your classroom. Chapter 2's moves will help create a smooth start with a new group of students on the first day of class. Chapters 3 and 4's moves continue to help you build strong relationships with students and also help students build friendly working relationships with one another. These chapters also include moves that will empower your students as they work with you to solve problems and refine the classroom community. Finally, Chapter 5 is the troubleshooting chapter. We are human and our students are human, and human relationships do not always run a predictable, conflict-free course. However, we can be prepared to bring our best selves to these situations so that we are doing our best to support our students. Part of this chapter offers moves that can proactively strengthen relationships with students and parents or guardians, and part of this chapter offers practical problem-solving moves for when you run up against a derailment. Once again, by working with students and parents or guardians, you empower all actors in problem-solving.

You'll notice that each move begins with a note about the immediate and long-term results of that move. I've included these notes as a reminder of the true effects of the work you do in the classroom each day. Everything we do as teachers is instructive to our students, even (perhaps especially) the things that we don't mean to teach them. Think back on your own experiences as a student: I'll bet you can still fondly remember a particular teacher's kindness or recall the sting of a teacher's cruelty from a lifetime ago. In the same way, the choices that we make in the classroom about whether to be collaborative or to require compliance leave an impression on our students. They affect students' behavior, students' motivation, and students' beliefs about themselves and their abilities in and beyond school. Remembering this long view can help us make decisions that are legitimately good for the students in our care, not just helpful in maintaining control in the moment.

If you've been a previous adherent to a "top-down" compliance model, don't be surprised if you feel uncomfortable turning the tables and inviting students to sit down at the management table with you. Any time we diverge from our practiced behaviors and routines, we feel discomfort. Therefore, embrace the discomfort; it means you are seriously moving in a direction that will ultimately improve your students' mastery and enjoyment of your content while reducing stress for your students and for you! And as you work to inhabit the moves of this book, ultimately internalizing them and making them your own, expect that the "Yellow Brick Road" will at times be bumpy. However, Dorothy never gave up when the road to her goal—returning home—got rough. Along the way, she recruited a team of supporters who were equally interested in meeting the "great and powerful Wizard of Oz." So take a tip from Dorothy: reaching a goal is easier when you have a team. Encourage your professional learning community (PLC) or your simpatico teacher colleagues to take this classroom management journey with you. While alone we often succumb to backsliding, demoralizing self-talk, and despair, a team offers refuge, an unjudging ear that listens and helps its members productively talk through problems and roadblocks so that you never forget the ultimate goal: your transformation into a teacher who routinely and consistently involves students in the management of their classroom community. The changes you make today will improve your students' learning and well-being every day they enter your classroom!

2

The First Few Days
INTRODUCING STUDENTS TO YOU AND ONE ANOTHER

Mark was a sophomore. He was very successful academically, yet also a bit shy. His voice had an unusual quality; to kids it would be defined as "sounding funny." His speech sometimes had a halting manner and in conversations he had to work hard to look directly at the speaker rather than beyond. Diagnosed as being on the autism spectrum, Mark had personal tics and quirks on the outside for all to see, whereas the rest of us have the luxury of hiding our quirks and tics from one another. A few weeks into the school year, I observed a group of girls teasing Mark. Because the remarks were not directed explicitly to Mark, he didn't pick up on what was going on, but the audience around the girls did. Boy, was I angry. However, I took a second to collect myself and tried instead to help the girls process their actions, their intent, and the effect of their behaviors.

After sending Mark on an errand that would take him out of the classroom for a good 10 minutes or so, I called the girls into the hallway and said, "I heard what you were saying in front of Mark. Did you stop to think about the impression you were sending to everyone else in the classroom with your words?"

The students didn't say much. One responded with a flat-voiced "I don't know." I continued, "Okay, since you haven't really thought this through, take a minute to do that now. If you're teasing someone in public, are other people likely to think that you're a kind person? Or will they think something else?"

More silence from the girls. I continued, "What was the intention of your behavior?"

The wheels of cognitive dissonance began to turn, outwardly manifested in silence while looking at the floor, fidgeting, and avoiding one another's glance. Soon they admitted that they did not want their classmates to view them as mean, insensitive individuals. This isn't unique to this group of kids: generally, people do not want others to think of them as mean. At this point, I asked them if they remembered how to behave in a friendly and supportive manner (see Chapter 3, page 72). They said they did. Last, I asked them if we needed to talk about this anymore, or were they clear on the classroom expectation that every person be treated in a respectful, positive way. One answered, "No, we get it," and the others nodded.

In subsequent days and weeks, Mark was treated respectfully, and classmates enjoyed working with him. His ideas were insightful, yet he never dominated a group, allowing others to share their ideas, too. Plus, by third quarter, when Mark had worked with many different classmates, enabling him to refine his own interpersonal skills, he had found the confidence to share a new side of himself: he had a great sense of humor!

A Word About Friendliness and Support

Throughout this book, we'll be discussing friendliness and support as major components of building a strong community. When people feel affirmed, valued, and cared about, they are more likely to bring their best selves to a situation. This is beneficial for students: they can let down their guard, focus on learning, and maybe even see school as enjoyable. This is beneficial for us: if the students in the room are generally friendly and supportive, it's easier for us to focus on their needs, strengths, and learning. This is beneficial for the class as a whole: the resulting calm provides a productive and pleasant environment.

But what happens if a student insults a peer? Or makes a comment tinged with sexism or bigotry? Is the student on the receiving end of a comment like these required to respond only in a friendly, supportive way? Of course not. If it looks as though a student needs your support, step in. An expectation of friendliness and support should never take precedence over an individual student's well-being.

Laying the Foundation for Friendliness, Support, and Collaboration

The hallway conversation about teasing occurred weeks into the school year, not on the first day of class. So why am I telling you this story as you prepare for the first day?

The answer is that what happens on the first day of school—and all the days after it—is the real reason why my conversation with the students was effective. By the time that conversation was necessary, I had worked with students to establish a classroom environment where all students could feel safe, appreciated, and respected. I had given them and their classmates opportunities to connect with one another, to be supportive as well as supported. So when I appealed to the students' understanding of those norms, they understood.

If I had tried to have that conversation without establishing that foundation first, I doubt it would have helped the situation: the students might not have thought there was anything wrong with their behavior. After all, Mark hadn't even noticed, right? They might have wondered what I was getting so upset about, laughed it off, and continued the teasing.

We can't wait until there's a problem to start laying that foundation. We have to start from the first moment of the first day.

The ideas in this chapter focus on offering ways to create a classroom with positive behavior expectations so that all students start the year feeling seen, safe, appreciated, and respected. Together these lessons lay out a plan for your first day (or your first few days, if you have shortened class periods). Often, a lesson or idea in this chapter builds upon earlier ideas. Therefore, you'll probably see your best success if you follow the moves in this chapter as a baker would follow a recipe, the final product being a classroom community foundation where students feel confident enough to take both academic and interpersonal risks, knowing that both teachers and students will support them.

GOAL	MOVES
Prepare for the First Day	• Decorate the Room, but Only a Little (page 21) • Plan the First Day (page 23) • Be Ready to Give Positive Attention (page 25) • Look Forward to Modeling Calmness, Respect, and Positivity (page 28)
Make the First Day Interesting, Inclusive, and Safe	• Greet Kids at the Door with a Warm Welcome (page 34) • Use a Novel, Unpredictable Method for Assigning Seats (page 36) • Take Attendance and Pronounce Names Correctly (page 40) • Introduce Yourself and Share the Day's Agenda (page 43)
Build Friendliness, Support, and Collaboration	• Establish Positive Behavior Norms Collaboratively (page 46) • Help Kids Get to Know You and One Another Through Interviewing (page 49) • Make Back-to-School Night Memorable (page 54)

Goal: Prepare for the First Day

Lessons to support this goal:

- Decorate the Room, but Only a Little (page 21)

- Plan the First Day (page 23)

- Be Ready to Give Positive Attention (page 25)

- Look Forward to Modeling Calmness, Respect, and Positivity (page 28)

TRADITIONAL APPROACH	COLLABORATIVE APPROACH
• Room décor is determined by the teacher, or room starts bare and stays bare. • Teacher demeanor is determined by mood while feedback veers toward what students are doing wrong versus what they are doing right.	• Room decoration emerges as student work is completed and displayed. • The teacher models positive behavior and positive feedback, the same behaviors expected from students.
⬇ LEADS TO ⬇	**⬇ LEADS TO ⬇**
Ø Teacher-determined décor sends the message that this is solely the teacher's space. Ø Students and teachers find themselves in opposition to one another and routinely face power struggles.	✔ Students feel greater ownership of the classroom when they can find a piece of their identity reflected in the space. ✔ Students are more likely to embrace positive norms in the context of daily interaction with others. They recognize that each classmate's behavior affects others.

Figure 2.1

MOVE>Decorate the Room, but Only a Little

Immediate Result: Your room will reflect just enough decoration to make the room inviting on the first day, but you will not have spent days on bulletin boards, time you could have spent more productively planning your first weeks' worth of lessons.

Long-Term Result: Your walls will evolve and fill with the work of your students. This display demonstrates you are proud of their work, but it also is a way for students to take a casual yet important interest in the work of their classmates in all your classes.

While a completely bare room can feel unusual on the first day of school, I think it's important not to overdecorate before students arrive. When setting up for the first day of class, aim to have just enough decoration for the room to feel welcoming but also enough "gallery space" for students to notice and say, "This room looks kind of bare." Which gives you the opportunity to respond, "Yes, you're absolutely right. We're going to have to work together to make this classroom look more inviting."

The most important wall enhancement you can display on that first day is a big welcoming banner or poster that says something like "We're glad you're here. Class wouldn't be the same without you!" This affirmation is really the cornerstone of the classroom community. We're all here to work together and appreciate everyone's unique talents and contributions. Be sure to place this banner or poster in a conspicuous spot where students will see it every day as they walk in. While everything else hung on your walls may evolve and change, this first-day banner should continue to hang in prominence until the end of the very last day (see Figure 2.2). It is *that* important!

Figure 2.2 Lauren Huddleston's door greets her seventh-grade students on the first day of the school year—and the last day of the school year.

Another piece of décor that can make a difference for students is a display of photos of a wide range of role models. Sports and entertainment figures may be the first to spring to mind, but push yourself to find authors, artists, scientists, political leaders, and humanitarians. The role models you post should represent a diverse array of people, ranging across gender, race, culture, and class. Every student should be able to see multiple successful people with whom they can identify. There's no need to complete this project before the year begins. Invite students to be curious about those who are posted and enlist their help in continuing the research you started, adding their own role models (Dibinga 2017).

The rest of your décor should be emergent. Rather than spend loads of time working on bulletin boards, use the walls to display student work. Ideally, the room should reflect the entire community, not your personal aesthetics. But don't worry, you'll have some great stuff hanging up in no time—students will be making posters and other displayable work in Chapters 3 and 4.

MOVE>Plan the First Day

Immediate Result: When you focus on your students, not on the fine print, students leave class on the first day thinking about establishing positive relationships and building community rather than on rules, requirements, looming assignments, and heavy textbooks.

Long-Term Result: From the first day, you've shown that this class will feature student-centered collaboration rather than teacher-centered performance. As students return day after day, the foundation has been laid for continued teamwork and refining collaboration skills.

As you make your plan, keep in mind one of my favorite first-day-of-school recommendations, which I learned through trial and error: save the syllabus and class rules for the *second week* of class. In the long run, beginning the year by building community helps kids learn the class rules through action, working with others, and practicing the respectful behavior that is modeled by the teacher. Kids will do what you do. And from a practical standpoint, as students pass from class to class, how many class policies can they absorb before their eyes glaze over and they tune out? We want students to look forward to returning the following day, not dread it.

Of course, as teachers, we immediately worry about when we will get to these "housekeeping" chores. Instead of piling them on that first day, think about how these items on your to-do list fit into context. On that first day, you could talk about the supplies needed for class so that students have the list and can go shopping for all their classes in one trip. On the other hand, maybe the time to talk about how you grade is a discussion to have prior to the first major assignment. Don't pass out the textbooks (or access codes for digital textbooks) until you are actually going to use them. And, if you use the textbooks sporadically, you might choose to have a classroom set as well as the books that you sign out to students. That way the books are there when you need them and no one has to return to their lockers because "that book is heavy and we haven't used it in weeks!" Your immediate supervisor may want to receive a copy of your class policies at the very beginning of the year, but that doesn't mean you have to spend that first period combing over them with your students. In the end, you might find that there are a lot of things you never have to talk about. And that's okay, because the community has created its own rules for functioning that might be even better than what you originally committed to paper.

MOVE>Be Ready to Give Positive Attention

> **Immediate Result:** Students will feel noticed and valued.
>
> **Long-Term Result:** If you expect that, over time, giving students positive attention will reinforce their sense of being noticed and valued, you're right. However, there's also another important benefit to this move: it helps *you* see your students in a positive light.

Giving students positive attention is important on the first day of school, but it isn't something that's limited to the first day of school—it's an important part of establishing rapport *every* day of the year.

The number of positive experiences linked to a student will significantly affect how you react in a moment of crisis involving that student. Building that upfront positive relationship will in turn minimize the likelihood that you will overreact if that student has a self-regulation lapse. And from the student/human perspective, people are a little less likely to engage in mean or disappointing behavior when they are invested in someone. It still might happen (people blow up at their loved ones from time to time), but since both parties have a relationship, it's much easier to repair the damage, solve problems that need to be solved, and talk about how to better work together in the future.

Setting a positive tone in the classroom benefits everyone in the room: for you, it means that the classroom is more likely to be productive and focused. For kids, it means that the classroom is more likely to be a place where they can focus on learning, a place where they can feel respected.

Without this feeling of safety, students may feel compelled to seek extra attention. In many situations, that means causing disruption.

When we look back on our own teaching experiences, the disruptive students are often the ones we remember years later. So, as long as we're going to remember those kids anyway, let's flip the script. Start giving consistent extra attention to those who seem to be in need of it. Notice positive things—a talent, an interest, an insightful comment—and strike up a quick conversation with them before class begins or just as they're leaving.

At the same time, resist the temptation to take personal offense at disruption. Instead, reframe these situations as opportunities for exercising your own compassion and leadership. Perhaps a well-timed disruption is more about a student trying to avoid an academic task that intimidates them than about challenging you personally. Or perhaps students are academically very capable but have trouble hiding their boredom. Offer lots of specific, positive feedback when these students do step up to the plate and make an effort. Show that you really noticed a precise content strength they demonstrated or a way they contributed to class. Also, there's nothing wrong with asking kids for advice about the class. Kids who are pushing against the structure of a class may well have devoted a great deal of class time to ongoing internal critiques of what's occurring in a classroom. Benefit from their expertise and make these kids your unofficial co-teachers. When these students develop a positive, rewarding relationship with you, their comfort and happiness will ripple outward, influencing the rest of the classroom community.

Figure 2.3 **Positive feedback need not be lengthy. These seventh graders are getting some positive comments as Lauren Huddleston sits in for a few minutes with each group.**

Part of being friendly and supportive is acknowledging that those you work with bring a wealth of talent and knowledge with them, and that you are eager to learn from them. Being a teacher isn't a one-way street.

If you are still feeling uncertain about how to connect with a student, there's nothing wrong with talking with their counselor, inclusion co-teacher, or any other adults in the building who might know them well. Sometimes simply demonstrating interest can help build a relationship (see Figure 2.3).

A few examples of useful comments:

- Thanks for sharing your idea about _____. That really got me thinking about _____.

- Your nails look great. Where do you get them done?

- Ms. _____ mentioned that you are a wonderful guitar player. I'm just starting. Got any advice for me?

- Yesterday when I watched you working with _____, you two were really getting into the conversation.

- I love the way you make people comfortable in your group. They are laughing but still get the work done.

- How do you like that book?

MOVE>Look Forward to Modeling Calmness, Respect, and Positivity

Immediate Result: When students see you treat everyone positively and respectfully, this will put them at ease, whether it's the first day of school, the last day of school, or any day in between.

Long-Term Result: When students are treated in ways that make them feel respected and valued, they are far more likely to model these behaviors in their interactions with you and their classmates.

It's impossible to anticipate every potential interaction you'll have with students as a teacher. However, if you can be calm, respectful, and positive in your interactions with students, you're likely on the right track. Following are some of the principles and suggestions that I've found most useful when it comes to my own demeanor in the classroom. I doubt you'll need to use all—or maybe any—of these on the first day of class, but I'm including them early in the book so that you have them ready when you need them, whenever that may be.

- **Teach your students how to accept a compliment.** For many students, their school day is not filled with positives, so consistently noticing their merits and giving positive feedback can actually make these students feel uncomfortable or suspicious. At the beginning of the school year, explain, "I really enjoy watching students at work and when I notice something great, it's something to celebrate and I'll want to say something to you. Don't worry, I won't single you out in front of the class. Even so, it makes some people uncomfortable, so they have a hard time receiving a compliment. If you're one of those people, the best way to overcome that awkward feeling is to say, 'Thanks for noticing.' Let's practice that.

Everybody turn to your partner, imagine you just got a compliment from them, and say, 'Thanks for noticing.'"

- **Interrupt your teaching by offering positive feedback.** At least 70 percent of the feedback we give students should be positive. While moving through the room, momentarily stop by, address a student by name, and quietly give that student a quick, instantaneous, positive, specific comment that attributes success to the student:

  - Thanks for pushing your backpack under the desk.

  - Great to see a fellow reader. Let me know later what you think of that book.

  - Your careful listening makes you a great partner.

  - Thanks for laughing at my joke.

  - I missed you yesterday; glad you're back.

  - Your idea about _____ really has me thinking.

  - I'm really interested in your puppy; later on in class I want you to give me an update.

  - That piece you wrote on your grandmother was great; it was like I met her.

  We often ignore positive behavior while targeting negative student behavior with laser precision. Believe it or not, the more negative feedback students receive, the more disruptive their behavior becomes (Fry 1983). Flip the script! Instead, keep the focus on giving students positive, warm feedback. And follow the succinct advice of educator Beverley Holden Johns (2018): "Be positive, be brief, be gone."

- **Offer positive feedback to the whole class.** Celebrate students who are working well together in their learning. Offer positives at the beginning and end of class that show you are noticing their efforts as a community. What might you say?

  - As I was watching you work in your groups today, I noticed everyone paying close attention to what their group members had to say and asking follow-up questions. We should post a video on YouTube so that other students can see what it looks like when groups are working together well.

- Look at that. Not a single person absent! Turn to your partner right now and thank them for coming to class today.

- Thanks for getting your materials out so quickly. I truly appreciate it when we can spend more time learning than waiting.

Keep the feedback warm, positive, and specific to that class. Describe what you saw rather than using generic, vague phrases such as "You all did a great job today. Keep up the good work!"

- **Use large-group discussions to dig deeper into the ideas hammered out in smaller groups.** Never ask questions you already know the answer to; this encourages students to try their best at mind reading, withdraw due to the risk of voicing a wrong answer, or, at worst, shout out irrelevant answers for attention or a laugh because they've realized the only correct answer is the one you already formulated. Instead, offer students questions that get them to think about material in original, open-ended ways. And then give students wait time (at least 10 seconds) to silently think or write. Before anyone can answer, make it clear that you will give the class an announcement or hand signal when the time is up. If we want students to really engage in higher-order thinking, it cannot occur in a matter of seconds (Benson 2014, 91).

- **Keep communication with students private.** Those quick positive or occasional redirecting comments are between you and the student; no one else should hear them. Also, if at least 70 percent of those private comments are positive, classmates will not automatically assume a student is in trouble when you offer a whisper to someone.

- **Explain to students that fairness and equity do not mean treating everyone exactly the same way.** Being fair and equitable means treating students as individuals and offering what each person needs in order to succeed. This is different from treating everyone equally. Treating people equally assumes that everyone is starting with the same advantages and background and therefore all require exactly the same kind of help.

- **Tell students that their privacy is important to you.** Sometimes students try to turn the blame on others. If a student says, "But Joanne is always talking in class," your reponse should be "We can discuss only your behavior. I will not discuss other students with you. And I promise that I will never discuss you with another student. Let me know when it is a good time for us to talk about you." Continue to repeat these sentences if necessary.

- **Memorize the "Student Strengths" section of a student's IEP.** Because we know that we are responsible for implementing the required accommodations in a student's IEP, it's not unusual for us to zoom in on that section of the document. While it's important to meet the listed accommodations, also give yourself time to focus on the IEP section labeled "Student Strengths," typically found at the very beginning of the summary. Resolve to work to that student's strengths as you implement the accommodations.

- **Admit when you're wrong.** We teachers are human too and make mistakes. Modeling a sincere apology is an important lesson for our students to see. On the flip side, *never* force an apology from a student. An insincere apology is no apology at all. Instead you might say, "I understand that you don't want to apologize, but, nevertheless, what you said/did was hurtful. I wonder how you can make this right. I'm interested in what action you might take."

- **Stay calm and speak in a low, even tone of voice.** Raising your voice to a student will be interpreted as a sign of aggression. So will finger-pointing and close proximity. In a pitched moment, it's okay to say to a student, "I'm too angry to talk about this now. Once I feel calmer, I'll be able to solve this problem with you in a respectful, adult manner."

Goal: Make the First Day Interesting, Inclusive, and Safe

Lessons to support this goal:

- Greet Kids at the Door with a Warm Welcome (page 34)
- Use a Novel, Unpredictable Method for Assigning Seats (page 36)
- Take Attendance and Pronounce Names Correctly (page 40)
- Introduce Yourself and Share the Day's Agenda (page 43)

TRADITIONAL APPROACH	COLLABORATIVE APPROACH
• The teacher superficially greets students at the door when it's convenient for the teacher. • Daily roll call verifies which students are present, but may not address issues such as mispronounced names or preferred names. • The seating chart is predetermined or students are allowed to choose seats.	• From the first day, the teacher prioritizes building relationships with students by offering positive, individual attention. • Students are seated in unpredictable ways. • Learning names is dealt with in a private, respectful manner. • First words from the teacher place an emphasis on developing relationships with one another.
⬇ LEADS TO ⬇	⬇ LEADS TO ⬇
∅ Alphabetical seating means students are more likely to be seated near the same classmates repeatedly. Allowing students to consistently choose seats can reinforce cliques and exclude others. ∅ Immediate, in-depth policy coverage results in information overload. Important rules will likely not be remembered. ∅ The teacher's self-introduction is hit-or-miss: some students might find it interesting while others might view it as a vanity lecture.	✔ Students feel acknowledged and appreciated as individuals. ✔ Randomized, often-updated seating creates opportunities to get to know all classmates.

Figure 2.4

The moves in the next section of this chapter will give you a clear structure for the first day (or, if you have shortened class periods, first few days) of class. To ensure that the day goes smoothly, get to know these moves, do the necessary prep work for each, and plan or even rehearse how you will implement them.

MOVE>Greet Kids at the Door with a Warm Welcome

Immediate Result: Providing every student with an enthusiastic hello offers them an impression of you as friendly, interested in each of them, and glad they'll be part of the class.

Long-Term Result: Continuing that daily greeting will have a positive impact on teacher–student relationships, enabling the kids to feel supported, comfortable, and respected every day as they walk in.

I'll admit, meeting students at the door is probably advice you've heard before, but it can be something that we *mean to* do more than we actually do. Whenever we have a spare moment, we teachers are tempted to get some work done: grade a paper, update attendance, adjust a bulletin board, or maybe just take a break and sit down. But at those moments when students are entering our classroom, the most important thing we need to do is stand by the door and greet them. Every day.

Now, think about *how* you're greeting students. On that first day it will be a smile and hello. Within the next week, up the ante to greeting each student by name as well as offering a quick positive anecdote—something you noticed about their learning, talents, contributions, or helpfulness (see Figures 2.5 and 2.6). The focus here is on letting the kids know that we see them and value them, not on barking out our own announcements or directions while they're walking in. Also, remember that no matter how enthusiastic we are, students may not automatically return our enthusiasm. You will have some kids who return an enthusiastic greeting and a few who walk right past you without acknowledgment. But that's okay. The point is you are there, you are visible, you are making the effort. Even for the kid who seems to be ignoring you, rest assured you are making a difference.

Figure 2.5 **Math teacher Ashley Boyd makes it a point to greet her students at the door with a handshake and a smile every single day. Of course, during flu season fist or elbow bumps are appropriate and welcome substitutions. And along with the smile, Ashley offers a quick exchange that might just include a hello, a comment on a previous day's success, or just a complimentary noticing. Anything that personalizes the moment for a student in a positive way is something worth saying.**

Figure 2.6 **Colleen Ghelfi makes a point to say good-bye to her students at the end of the period, offering them some quick positive feedback based on an observation she made during the period.**

MOVE> Use a Novel, Unpredictable Method for Assigning Seats

Immediate Result: Students will know that there is a place for them as soon as they walk in and that they don't need to worry about the influence of cliques and prior friendships as they take a seat. Plus, the stress on students brand-new to your school, who have no prior acquaintances, is reduced when they are not the only ones working with someone they don't know well.

Long-Term Result: From the first day forward, students will understand that your goal is to provide them the opportunities to get to know and work with all their classmates. Also, as students work with those whom they do not know well, they become more socially skilled as well as expand their acquaintanceship to include classmates who might be different from those in their usual friendship circle. The only way for students—and adults—to break through their preconceived biases is to move beyond superficial acquaintance and really get to know one another.

Should we let students pick their own seats or assign them? While letting students choose their own seats may sound more democratic, the sad truth is that experiments with "general admission" seating often result in high levels of distracting, off-task conversation. And then, if that issue goes unresolved after numerous redirections and individual chats, students doubly resent it when we step in and reassign their seats. As author and educator Eric Toshalis (2015) explains:

> *The truth is, open seating isn't democratic, doesn't support student autonomy, and seldom teaches students to self-regulate. The tiny uptick in self-rule a student might experience when choosing a desk is quickly eclipsed when that student must search for the least dangerous seat amid adversaries, bullies, cliques, and even crushes that are always operating in our classrooms. Open seating allows the worst parts of those phenomena to fester. That stresses kids out.*

"But my students plead for open seating," you say? Of course they do—or at least some of them do. Keep in mind that those who broadcast their desire to sit next to their friends may be doing so to flaunt the fact that they have the richest social network, may feel entitled to have a classroom dedicated to their desires, and may believe that others can fend for themselves in determining where to sit. Instead of yielding to the more dominant voices in the room, look at your classroom from the perspective of the marginalized. Think of the new kid who mistakenly sits in a popular student's seat and is mocked for doing so. Or imagine the student who was meeting with a counselor to discuss a difficult life issue only to come to class late and be forced to find a desk while surrounded by snickering peers.

Additionally, in adult life we are *always* thrust into situations where we must become acquainted and work with people we don't know, so it behooves us to give students opportunities to work with students they don't know and to teach students how to navigate new relationships successfully (which will be addressed in detail in the next chapter).

Let's think about how we can make this process supportive of students on that first day.

Many teachers just automatically fall back on alphabetical order by last name. That organization has a lot of pluses: it's predictable, it matches the attendance list, and it might make it easier for you to learn names and pass back papers in the beginning of the year. The downside is that many students find themselves sitting near the same kids year after year. At the very least, sitting by the same kids limits new friendship opportunities. But worse, it can create a situation where a bullying victim is repeatedly forced to sit near a perpetrator. Imagine what it would be like to sit year after year directly in front of a student who never stops poking you in the back or is adept at whispering nasty things in your ear when the teacher is beyond earshot.

This year try taking a small risk and seat students in a less predictable way on that very first day. You might try the following strategies:

- Number the desks and create corresponding numbered index cards. As students walk in, flair the cards like you're in Vegas. Keep the numbers hidden. Each student pulls a card and finds the corresponding desk number. Once everyone is seated, collect the cards and use them again for the next class.

- Another way to randomly pair students up in the beginning of the year is with the use of objects, an idea from high school teacher Colleen Ghelfi (see Figure 2.7). Colleen explains the process:

> Clean out your desk drawer and find matched pairs: two erasers, two pennies, two of the same pens, etc. When kids walk in, have them pick something out of the bowl/bucket/box. It's fun to watch them choose: some kids grab anything while others are very picky. When they ask why they are picking an object, just say, "You'll see." Once class begins, have kids find their "object match" partner and then have them sit down together side by side.

Once seats are assigned, immediately teach students this "housekeeping" routine: stowing their stuff under their desks or in another part of the room to make it easy to move around the room. Establishing this norm now means that you won't have to

Figure 2.7 **Colleen Ghelfi found these random pairing items in her desk.**

remind them about it quite as often in the coming days and you'll be free to roam the room. If space is tight, consider how you might reorganize the room to make it easier to navigate. If tight spaces can't be avoided, teach students how to "pull in" and make room when someone is passing through an aisle.

Assure students that their seats will change regularly. Rotate student seating at least every three or four weeks. Depending on your students and their needs, you might change seats more frequently. And when you create a new seating chart, remember to also give students opportunities to sit in different areas of the room. By the time students leave your room at the end of the year or semester, they should have had opportunities to meet and work with as many classmates as possible.

While randomized, frequently changed seating is beneficial in many situations, let yourself make exceptions when necessary. If a student's IEP specifies a particular seating requirement, honor it. If a student raises a seating concern with you, listen and adjust accordingly. You can make these adjustments without fanfare the next time the class meets, speaking to the students privately to ask them to make a switch. If students ask for a reason for the change, a reminder that you'll be moving seats a lot in this class and a simple comment such as "It's always good to mix things up" can help you move things along when it's not appropriate to delve into the reasons for the change publicly.

MOVE>Take Attendance and Pronounce Names Correctly

Immediate Result: Working in a systematic way to learn how to correctly pronounce each student's name shows respect and prevents embarrassing moments for you and your students.

Long-Term Result: Using correct pronunciation shows students you value them and their identity, and it averts the kind of harm that kids face when their names are consistently mispronounced. Cavalier, insensitive mispronunciations truly do influence students' self-identity, as education researcher Punita Chhabra Rice (2017) points out. "Research has found that students' socioemotional well-being and worldview can be negatively impacted by teachers' failure to pronounce their names properly, and can even lead students to shy away from their own cultures and families." Plus, using names is part of the ongoing work of building positive relationships. Students whose names are consistently mispronounced feel disrespected and rendered invisible (Mitchell 2016).

Once students take their seats, it may seem like a good time to take attendance. But hold off on that for a minute. Instead, pass out index cards.

Now it's time to get your students to help you pronounce their names correctly and address them in the way they want to be addressed.

The official class roster that I have shows most of your names in their formal versions, but listening to you greet your friends as you came in, I heard many of you use different versions of those formal first names and some of you used nicknames. Take a moment and think about which first name you want everyone in this class to use when they address you.

Grab that card I gave you and neatly print your first and last names. Then take a look at what you've written. Is the first name you wrote down the one that you really want everyone in this class to address you by? If not, change your first name on the card.

Now, write your name again phonetically. This means that you will spell it out so that I can understand how to pronounce it correctly and put emphasis on the right syllables.

Demonstrate with the phonetic spelling you use for your own name. Say it out loud, so that students can hear where the emphasis and syllable breaks are, and match the sounds with the phonetic version you've written. The goal of the phonetic spelling is to accurately show you how to pronounce a student's name correctly. Whatever spelling conveys this most clearly is the correct way; there is no need to stop and teach a lesson on the pronunciation key in *Webster's Dictionary* (see Figure 2.8).

While students are working, give them a hand if they are stuck, but also encourage them to reach out to others near them for help or a second opinion. Take a walk down the rows, quickly reviewing the cards with students. Of course, some of the names will be familiar to you and will have pronunciations you already recognize, but still quietly say each name aloud to confirm it with each student. As you make your way through the class, take the day's attendance, as well.

For the names that challenge you, carefully review the phonetic spelling. Kids are not phonetic experts, so notes can be unintentionally inaccurate or misleading. If you find you are pronouncing a student's name incorrectly, work together to revise the phonetic spelling so that it offers you better cues. But also, immediately apologize for not getting it right. Continue by underscoring that names are important and you might need a little more help from that student. While you are confirming name

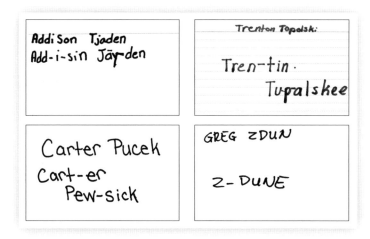

Figure 2.8 **As long as a student has conveyed how to correctly pronounce their name, then the phonetic spelling choices are correct.**

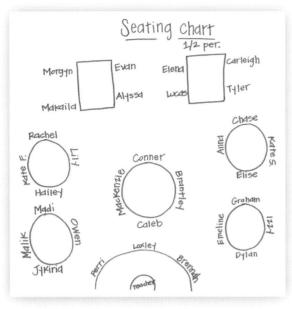

Seating chart
1/2 per.

Morgyn · Evan
Makaila · Alyssa
Elena · Carleigh
Lucas · Tyler

Rachel
Kate F. · Lily
Hailey
Madi
Malik · Owen
J'Kiria

Conner
MacKenzie · Brantley
Caleb
Loxley
Perri · Brennah
Teacher

Chase
Anna · Kate S.
Elise
Graham
Emeline · Izzy
Dylan

Figure 2.9 Here is one of Lindsey Jones' first-day-of-school seating chart, created as she conferred individually with students to review their pronunciation cards.

pronunciations, you can also fill in a seating chart. Creating a seating chart in real time on the first day will enable you to learn names even more quickly (see Figure 2.9). Also, if you find a few of your students' names challenging, do not hesitate to write in the phonetic spellings as well. "Official" seating charts are especially helpful for early in the year name help, as well as when an unexpected emergency arises and a substitute must captain the ship.

Aim to learn your students' names as quickly as possible. Each day that a kid realizes that you don't know their name is a day when that kid doesn't feel like a priority to you. Do whatever works for you to facilitate this. A few ideas:

- "Make attendance charts right away," says seventh-grade teacher Lindsey Jones. Using an attendance chart, not an attendance list, will help you match names to faces.

- If your school attendance program includes photo rosters as well as lists of names, use them to help you match names to faces. If not—or if the photos are out-of-date—you might ask students for permission to take photos of them on that very first day, perhaps with them holding their name cards up so that you can easily match their faces and names. Do not share these photos—they're only for your own reference.

MOVE> Introduce Yourself and Share the Day's Agenda

Immediate Result: During the first few minutes of class, quickly introducing yourself and previewing the agenda and baseline expectations can allay student anxieties and bring them on board. It will help them see that everything is happening for a reason rather than a whim. As you address the class, be yourself but understand that your role is to reassure and persuade your students that this will be a great class for all of you.

Long-Term Result: Students can trust that, in your class, planning is evident, their need for social connection is taken into consideration, and there is a predictable yet also novel routine to each day.

This beginning of the very first class should last only a couple of minutes. After telling the class how delighted you are to be working with them this year, put your name on the board and write it phonetically so that you can show how to pronounce it correctly (this is modeling for an activity they will do later, which was described in the previous move). You don't need to say a lot about yourself right now: you'll have a chance to share a bit of personal information later in the class (see Help Kids Get to Know You and One Another Through Interviewing on page 49).

Have everyone check their schedules and make sure they are in the right class at the right time. Inevitably, at least one student in the course of that first day will be in the wrong place. Most likely, that student will already be up and running to the correct location, but, before they go, warmly and genuinely thank them for trying to attend your class, tell them you look forward to working with them in the future, ascertain that they know where they should be, and have a pass ready so that they aren't marked tardy to their real class.

What else should you immediately tell your class in those first moments?

1. In this class, you can expect to get know everyone else in class. But don't worry, I'll be planning ways for you to get better at working together.

2. Working with those we don't know well is interesting because they have different perspectives and insights. That's why we already mixed it up with your seating.

3. I'm looking forward to getting to know and working with all of you.

4. Everything we do in here we do for a specific reason. If you ever wonder about a teacher decision I've made, please ask.

What else might be helpful? Getting into the habit of projecting or listing the day's agenda will help students prepare for each class as they organize their materials and their minds. On the first day point out the agenda, and encourage students to take a look at it every day as they enter the room.

Monday, August 17, 2020

- Welcome!
- Schedule Check
- Fire Drill Info
- Supplies
- How would you like to be remembered?
- Partner Interviews

HW: Supplies DUE Tuesday, August 25

Figure 2.10 **Posting an agenda from the very first day forward helps students prepare mentally as well as physically as they see what materials they will need for the day.**

Figure 2.10 shows an example of a first-day agenda. Notice that it hints at a busy schedule yet also provides a few mysteries that will make students curious. While there are some housekeeping chores you should not ignore on the first day—explaining fire drill procedures and providing a supply list (along with ample time for shopping)—those chores are targeted and brief. As we discussed earlier in Plan the First Day, keeping the chores minimal is intentional.

Goal: Build Friendliness, Support, and Collaboration

Lessons to support this goal:

- Establish Positive Behavior Norms Collaboratively (page 46)
- Help Kids Get to Know You and One Another Through Interviewing (page 49)
- Make Back-to-School Night Memorable (page 54)

TRADITIONAL APPROACH	COLLABORATIVE APPROACH
• Rules and expected norms are spelled out and predetermined by the teacher. • Introductions mostly focus on the teacher talking about themselves. • The back-to-school night presentation focuses on rules, expectations, and the syllabus.	• Students begin to identify positive classroom norms by thinking about how they would like others to remember them. • The teacher and students learn about one another through active interviewing, showing genuine interest and care for one another. • Back-to-school night offers parents and guardians the opportunity to experience a content-area minilesson.
⬇ LEADS TO ⬇	⬇ LEADS TO ⬇
∅ Students take on the roles of semi-anonymous workers, who may or may not feel safe or appreciated, and who do not feel a sense of community within the classroom. ∅ Students feel little ownership in rules and norms. Teacher and students feel disconnected and isolated from one another. ∅ By the end of back-to-school night, individual teacher presentations become blurred and indistinguishable. Parents and guardians don't feel a connection to the teacher.	✔ Students immediately begin to understand the importance of working together, developing positive working relationships with one another as well as with the teacher. ✔ Students take ownership and respect classroom norms since they had a significant role in creating them. ✔ Parents and guardians remember the class positively and consequently are more likely to support the teacher.

Figure 2.11

MOVE>Establish Positive Behavior Norms Collaboratively

Immediate Result: Giving students an opportunity for self-reflection on the very first day enables them to start the year or semester with a clear idea of what success looks like. A first-day prompt that focuses on what matters to students offers yet another way to set a student-centered tone. Also, just a couple of minutes to think and write can have a calming effect on students. (It can also give you the opportunity to calm your own first-day jitters with some cleansing deep breaths since your students' eyes are off you and on their writing.)

Long-Term Result: The piece that students write, though short, offers you a writing sample from each student, something that can inform early instructional decisions. Plus, periodically students can track their own growth by returning to these early thoughts and reflecting upon their contributions to the community.

Make your first assignment something that emphasizes positive norms. This activity, "How Would You Like to Be Remembered?," has proven useful for years in my class and in the classes of my colleagues.

Pass out index cards or half sheets of paper to students. Ask them to put their name at the top, and then pose this prompt or project it on the board:

> Since you'll be working with a variety of people over the school year, how will you consistently make a good first impression? What will you do? How will you act? What will you say? How do you want to be remembered? Take a minute to jot down some ideas that come to mind. Make a list. Don't worry about using complete sentences or correct spelling. Just get your ideas down on the card. For example, I might write down . . . "friendly, organized, helpful."

If some students remind you that they already know everybody and that the impressions are already made, just remind them that this is a new year, which always offers the opportunity of presenting ourselves in a brand-new light. Give students a quick minute or two to jot a few words and phrases. Then collect the cards and ask students to quietly listen while you read some of their thoughts aloud without mentioning anyone's names. End by showing your faith in the class, perhaps with something like "I can tell this is going to be a great year because all of you are so in tune with how to make a first impression. And this is going to come in handy because in just a few more minutes you'll be working together for real, so don't forget what you wrote down!" And if you run across any "snarky" responses, those students are sending you a strong "I need your attention" message; take heed and work on offering them some custom positive, thoughtful noticings that may help smooth those first-day bristles.

Here's another way to use this activity. Middle school teacher Jenna Leser starts by displaying negative descriptors that most people *wouldn't* want to be remembered for (see Figure 2.12). While the students are writing about how they *do* want to be remembered, Jenna erases the negative words. Once students have some ideas on their cards, Jenna invites students up a row or so at a time to grab a marker and add a positive trait

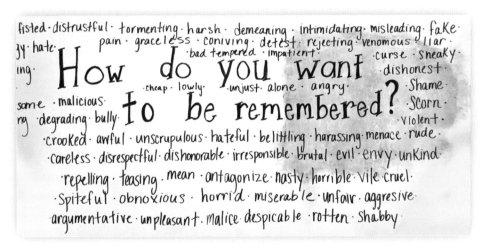

Figure 2.12 **When students walk into the room, the board is filled with negative descriptors, words and phrases that students—most likely—would not want to be remembered for.**

or two to the board. And then once everyone has contributed, Jenna takes a photo that the class can revisit throughout the year, long after the whiteboard has been erased (see Figure 2.13). What do you do with the cards after that? You could pick a few every day to hold in your hand while greeting students. When a card holder comes by, start up a quick impromptu conversation by asking who inspired them to write down that characteristic. You'll likely get to hear about their coaches, former teachers, parents, relatives, siblings, neighbors. Pretty interesting stuff!

Be sure to save the cards even after you've exhausted their doorway chat potential. Periodically, pass them back to students and have them reflect on their own classroom behavior as it compares to their original first-day thoughts. Are there positive traits they could add that they have expressed when working with others? Are there traits that are pretty important but they've forgotten about? How do they want their classmates to remember them when the year ends, and what are they doing to ensure those positive memories?

Figure 2.13 **There are lots of positive ways to be remembered by others!**

MOVE>Help Kids Get to Know You and One Another Through Interviewing

Immediate Result: The students will have an opportunity to find out the things about you that are of most interest to them, and you won't have to bore them with introducing yourself.

Long-Term Result: Collecting the interest surveys offers you another window into each student's world that will help you build relationships. Likewise, making interviewing a part of your classroom routine (see Chapter 3 for more about interviewing throughout the year) will help students build community with one another.

Begin by letting students know that they'll be filling out an interest inventory—a page that will help others get to know them. Be clear that what they write is for sharing with you and with the class. Then provide your own completed inventory as a model. Let students study it for a minute and then use your example to help them understand what your expectations are for the survey: "Notice that when I responded, my answers weren't super long, but I tried to answer all the items with some specific details. I'll leave this up as an example."

Then go ahead and pass out the inventory, giving students a few minutes to fill it out while you work on learning their names silently.

I've used the following survey shown with success, but you can also create your own. A few ideas to keep in mind when designing an interest survey:

- Limit the number of items to about ten or twelve: enough to get a variety of ideas, but not so many that the task becomes overwhelming.

- Leave plenty of white space around the items for additional writing later.

Choose topics about which students have sufficient background knowledge. Also, choose topics that serve as common denominators for the class. For example, instead of asking about a favorite vacation (which makes the assumption that everyone's families go on vacation), ask about a place you would like to visit. For this activity, aim for low-risk items that students would feel comfortable sharing with others: items that are non-controversial, fun, interesting, and engaging (see Figure 2.14 and Online Resource 2.1). Once the students have completed the inventories, it's time to begin modeling how to listen and ask follow-up questions.

Background/Interest Survey

Name _____

Date _____ Hour _____

1. Places you've lived

2. Pets you've had or would like to have

3. Favorite music artist/group and song

4. Place you would like to visit

5. Out-of-school pursuits/hobbies

6. Favorite subject other than this class!

7. Languages you speak or would like to learn

8. Favorite foods

9. Best place to get a haircut

10. Favorite SCHOOL-APPROPRIATE YouTube video

11. Favorite holiday

12. Household chores: Which ones are okay? Which ones do you hate?

Figure 2.14 **Sample Interest Inventory**

Start by returning to your own completed interest survey. Let students study it again and then ask them which topic they'd like to interview you on. Pick whichever one gets shouted the loudest. Then introduce the interview process by saying,

> When you are conducting an interview, it is of the utmost importance to put the interview subject at ease and never pose a question that might intentionally or accidentally embarrass them. If we were conducting an interrogation in a courtroom or if we were reporters questioning public figures about their actions, we might ask uncomfortable questions or insist that the person answer our questions. But that's not what we're doing now. Here, if a person declines to answer a question or expresses discomfort with a question or topic, accept that and move on. A good interviewer is always sensitive to the feelings of the subject.
>
> Based on that important idea, what's a question you could ask me to get a little more information on the topic?

Pick a question from the students, answer it, and then ask for another question. If you're asked a question that you'd rather not answer or that makes you uncomfortable, respond honestly: your response will be a model for students if they find that someone asks them something they don't want to respond to. You might say, "You know, that's something that I'd rather not talk about. Is there something else you might ask me instead?"

Repeat this question-answer pattern until students have asked enough follow-up questions to have elicited sufficient topic elaboration from you. Then ask the students to name some of the strategies that worked for them as an interviewer. Point out any of the important aspects of interviewing they might have missed. For example, helpful strategies for interviewing include

- Listen carefully and ask questions based on the partner's answers.
- Ask questions that require more than a one-word answer.
- Stick with the same topic until you've really found out about it.
- Do not interject your own thoughts, experiences, or ideas into the interview. The interviewer's job is to focus on getting information from the interview subject.

And, when being interviewed, it's helpful to

- Listen carefully to the interview questions.
- Answer with specific details that give the interviewer a path to further questions.

Now match each student with a partner and ask partners to trade interest inventories. Tell students to read the inventories and pick out four topics they would like to interview their partner on. Then let them take turns interviewing each other on the topics they've chosen. Upon the conclusion of the interviewing, remember to collect and save the interest surveys for later use.

If you have time, Colleen Ghelfi, a tenth-grade teacher in Tinley Park, Illinois, has found a great way to combine interviewing with sketchnoting.

After students have picked out the topics they want to interview their partners on, I pass out blank sheets of paper and tell the kids to fold the paper so that they have four boxes. In the center, students write their partner's first name. I remind students to use good interviewing skills, which means getting lots of details. But here's the catch: they have to take notes during their interviews without *using words because this challenges the students to focus only on visual representation [see Figure 2.15]. They have to think in a different way. Of course, if they slip and use a few words, I'm not going to make a big deal about it. I show the kids some examples from former students so they understand what to do. Finally, I have nearby pairs combine to form groups of four. In their new groups (with whom they will be working together in future classes), each kid has to introduce and talk about their partner using the sketchnotes [see Figure 2.16]. It feels a bit chaotic, but it's also a lot of fun.*

Figure 2.15 When interviewing her partner, Sydney, Tara found out that Sydney loves going to the beach. After graduation, she's looking forward to going to college and eventually becoming a doctor.

Figure 2.16 **This group of sophomores just finished introducing their members to one another and are celebrating their new partnership with some high fives, at their teacher's request.**

Figure 2.17 **Practice makes perfect! Also, notice how the student on the right has just turned himself around rather than moving the entire desk. This enables partners to work together more closely, which results in better focus and quieter voices, a gift to teachers in adjoining rooms when their students are silently reading or taking a test.**

Do the kids in Figure 2.16 look as though this is not their idea? Yes, a little. But, believe it or not, that doesn't mean it's not working. As artificial as these initial high fives might look, they are a start. When teaching any new social skill (even celebration), that skill usage will move through four stages (Johnson, Johnson, and Holubec 2008). First, they may be *reluctant* to try the skill: you'll need to remind them to use it. Next, they may use the skill, perhaps even without a prompt, but it might still be *awkward* or a little stiff. But, after a while, kids actually buy into the skill, realizing that it makes their collaboration more effective and fun—this is when you might see *overuse* of the skill. In the case of high fives, you might witness group members high-fiving one another *every* time a member makes a contribution. Finally, students *integrate* the skill, using it appropriately. This is when you'll see group members recognizing a celebratory moment and initiating a high five without your prompt (see Figure 2.17).

MOVE>Make Back-to-School Night Memorable

Immediate Result: Families will find the 10 minutes they spend with you during open house interesting and enjoyable.

Long-Term Result: A family's goodwill can in turn influence a student to think positively about your class. A positive response from families lays the foundation for further communication. Research shows that family involvement with school is linked to higher academic achievement. Additionally, a strong relationship with families can be invaluable should you ever need to contact them about a concern ("Parent, Family, Community Involvement" 2008).

As we are planning for the first day of class, we might be blindsided by another type of first-day event: back-to-school night. Yet this evening is just as important in developing a collaborative classroom as the first day of classes is.

It's become common practice for teachers to spend each 10-minute period of back-to-school night reviewing that class' syllabus, homework, and grading standards. While it may be tempting to continue this tradition—after all, isn't this important information?—stop to remember why we don't do this with our students on the first day of school: the syllabus parade is overwhelming, impersonal, and ineffective. After an evening of visiting a full day's schedule of classes, who would be able to remember your class' particular grading structure or late policy? Yes, of course share pertinent information with families, but might that be in a handout they can examine later or on a syllabus that is emailed to all families or posted on your part of the school website? If indeed these sources of class information can be shared elsewhere, then I propose you use your 10-minute period to offer parents and guardians a taste of your class. What might you do? Here are a few options.

Feature Each Class in a PowerPoint

Throw together a PowerPoint presentation that features each individual class. Take some great photos of each class in action: working in groups, working with partners, working individually, participating in class activities. Then pop these photos into separate PowerPoint shows. There is no need for any text since you are the narrator explaining the activities as the photos are displayed. Parents and guardians really do love seeing their students in action; just make sure you have photos that feature everyone. Your narration can give families an idea of what's happening in your class academically, as well: "Here, you can see Ben and Avery interviewing each other early in the school year. They're building skills that we'll be using later this month in our upcoming community research project."

Create Your Wall of Support

If you have time to have students complete the Home Court and Friendliness and Support moves in Chapter 3 (see pages 79–81 and 92–95) before back-to-school night, you can use the students' posters to introduce parents and guardians to the important relationship maintenance skills you're working on in class (see Figure 2.18). During the open house, explain the posters and the class behavior norms they represent. All parents and guardians want their children to feel safe, appreciated, and respected, so spending a few minutes explaining your "wall of support" is worthwhile. If you time it right, you can use the remaining 5 minutes for a quick partner activity: conducting interviews or possibly

Figure 2.18 **Invite students to help get the classroom ready for open house by hanging the work they've created.**

sharing ideas about a very short passage or poem related to your content. Partners can each take a turn sharing or interviewing, but save another minute for your attendees to return their gaze to the posters, finding a concrete Home Court or Friendliness and Support example that they can thank their partner for using.

Teach a Tiny Piece of Content in an Engaging Way

Letting families experience what it's like to be a student in your classroom—even briefly—will help them see how you're building a community with your students. What's something in your content that you could teach interactively in 10 minutes and that parents and guardians would find useful?

- The fashion design teacher teaches her parents and guardians how to sew on a button.
- The health teacher passes out food labels to parent and guardian partners to examine and leads a mini-discussion on how to decipher them.
- An English teacher projects an accessible short poem. After parent or guardian pairs discuss their favorite words and lines, the teacher invites partners to think and talk together about incidents from their own lives that would make good poems.
- A math teacher passes out two graphs on the same topic. Parent or guardian pairs examine, discuss, and decide which graph is more persuasive and which graph is more accurate. Voilà, a quick lesson on statistics!
- The social studies teacher pairs up the parents and guardians and teaches them how to argue both sides of an issue using a topic that often comes up at home.

Those are just some examples. If you are stumped for a good minilesson, ask your students. By the time back-to-school night rolls up, they will have been working with you for a couple of weeks, so they will have suggestions.

No matter which option you choose, the end goal for open house is the same: to give families a positive feeling about your class and to open the door for further communication.

Are You Ready?

- ☐ You've determined how to assign seats and prepared any necessary materials.

- ☐ You're ready to greet your students at the door and refuse to get distracted by your email, attendance corrections, or smartphone.

- ☐ You've rehearsed (at least in your head) how you will introduce yourself and share the day's agenda.

- ☐ You're ready to give attention in positive ways—especially to the students who need a little extra attention.

- ☐ You've reviewed your class policies and other "chores," decided which can wait to be discussed, and rehearsed how to discuss those remaining.

- ☐ You've experimented with phonetically spelling your own name as well as a few others so that you can explain this task to students.

- ☐ Your interest inventory is filled out and ready for projection, you've rehearsed (in your head) explaining how to be an interviewer, and you're ready to be an interview subject.

- ☐ You are ignoring the self-talk that's telling you any change in past opening day routine is going to fail. Celebrate your risks. No change occurs without imperfection. Embrace it.

How's It Going?

Once the day is over, try this quick reflection. This assessment is meant only for you. On a scale from one to ten, with one being "little student talk" and ten being "mostly student talk," how would you assess that first classroom period?

Building the foundation of a classroom community starts with valuing all voices and collectively working together. Building a classroom foundation of compliance means keeping the teacher front and center. Based on the score you just gave yourself, was the day more about building community or about building a foundation of compliance?

A basic tenet of community is sharing the stage. The more you give your students the opportunity to initiate the action, create the conversation, and take responsibility for classroom proceedings, the more likely they are to be invested, because you are showing them in real ways that their presence affects and influences the learning and social interactions of the class. This is a group endeavor rather than a teacher acting solo as the intrepid leader with thirty "campers" dutifully marching in line behind. If you find yourself focusing more on your actions or comments than on your students when you recall your day, think about how you can move from being a "sage on the stage" to being a "guide on the side." And no, this move does not mean you are abdicating your role of teacher. You are carefully and strategically structuring experiences and interactions for students that will help them grow as learners, thinkers, and collaborators.

If, today, you ended up on the low end of the scale, what might you try to do a little differently on subsequent days? If you ended up on the high end, how will you sustain this talk shift instead of gradually drifting back into a more teacher-directed dynamic?

3

The First Few Weeks of School

DEEPENING CONNECTIONS AND STRENGTHENING NORMS

Andy, a sophomore, struggled to pass his classes and stay in the good graces of his teachers due to a temper. Other teachers had warned me about his meltdown potential: angry outbursts that began with a fusillade of foul language directed at the teacher and ended when Andy exited the room, slamming the door behind him. I walked a high wire daily, ever expecting his frustration with the academic work to erupt with volcanic intensity. My bell to bell Andy anxiety continued until I discovered he was the *only* person who could reliably repair the string of holiday lights that festooned the classroom. Every day they conked out, and every day at the beginning of third period Andy patiently repaired the light string, jiggling the wires, methodically checking the individual bulb connections, and finding and replacing a burned-out bulb when warranted. And every day as I thanked Andy for his expertise at lighting up the bulbs again, I marveled at his understanding of the problem and the care he took to diagnose and fix it. A defective string of lights helped Andy and me bond while the rest of the class became increasingly impressed that anyone could make a broken string of holiday lights work time and again. No one had ever seen anyone do that! Andy's previously hidden talent enabled him to garner the esteem of his peers. In the end, Andy passed the class and I pitched that string of lights: I knew there would never be another Andy to fix them each day.

Susan, a high school junior, was another student who had trouble getting along with other teachers and students. She had difficulty connecting with teachers or classmates because others perceived her as being in a perpetually bad mood. She frowned a lot. Plus, she was short on patience and quick to "cuss someone out" if another's actions displeased her. However, early on I found that she truly enjoyed being helpful. Susan would dependably volunteer to hole-punch or staple papers, organize handouts, or run errands. Since she came in on her free time to get things ready for me, we had the chance to chat as she worked. I found out about her family and her dogs, and that if you only drink bottled water growing up, you'll get more cavities because the bottled water isn't fluoridated (who knew?). Susan also gave me another piece of health advice: if you want to avoid strep throat, *never* drink out of the school water fountains! I'm not sure if any hard facts backed up that claim, but after I took Susan's advice, I never came down with another case of strep throat. In exchange, I talked with Susan about my teaching decisions—why I chose certain activities and strategies over others, why I felt it was so important for students to work together in collaborative groups. Over the course of the year, while Susan helped me, she gradually became more adept at working with others. Of course, Susan wasn't perfect; none of us are. She still had an occasional meltdown and shouted some words she regretted. But here's the thing: because we had a relationship, I didn't take it personally or blow it out of proportion. And after a blowup, Susan recognized her error. Early in the year, Susan blamed her rages on her teachers and classmates, but as her classroom connections strengthened, she began taking responsibility for her actions, apologizing to those affected, and resolving to do better.

Making Connection a Priority

Andy's and Susan's stories show just how much a student's sense of connection—to teachers *and* to peers—affects their investment in class. By making it a priority to learn about our students' strengths and talents, we can help students recognize gifts their classmates bring to the table, further strengthening the community.

Even if you agree with me on those points, I know that now that you're a couple of weeks into the school year, you might be tempted to cut a few corners when it comes to community building and to spend more time on content and academic skills. It's understandable, especially if things have been going passably well in class. Isn't everything fine?

Here's where it's important to keep at this work, even if everything seems fine at the moment. Letting community building fall by the wayside (or expecting that it will take care of itself) communicates to students—rightly or wrongly—that how they treat you and each other is not a priority in your classroom. So, when something comes along that might test the tranquility of your classroom—a student having a legitimately bad day, an argument in your class, a disagreement about a grade—you'll find that you have no foundational relationship to fall back on. This is why so many teachers find themselves sounding like the authoritarian teachers they disliked when they were students: when the teacher is running a classroom alone, instead of managing a classroom together with students, the only tool at the teacher's disposal is their authority. Don't let yourself be caught in this situation.

If the pressure of time is still on your mind, remember that the time you spend now building a strong foundation of respect, interest, and mutual cooperation will save you time later when students can conduct themselves confidently and independently as they collaborate together.

The ideas and moves in this chapter all focus on helping further build relationships: between student and teacher as well as among students. Also found in this chapter are ways to help students develop, invest in, and uphold positive classroom norms. Emphasizing relationships and positive norms into the first weeks of school shows students that you are serious about a collaborative, supportive, friendly classroom. It also gives you and the students more opportunities to get to know each other and to strengthen your interpersonal skills.

But the moves in this chapter have another superpower: they help us, the teachers, be more effective in challenging moments. I've yet to meet a strong teacher who doesn't recall a situation in the classroom that they wished they'd handled differently: a time when they realized too late that they had come down too hard, had escalated a situation, or had let their own embarrassment or anger take over. When we, the adults in the room, feel a strong connection to the kids as individuals and as human beings, we're far less likely to make those mistakes.

As in the previous chapter, a later move often builds upon an earlier one. However, in this chapter you can use the moves a bit more flexibly, choosing those that best meet your needs and the needs of your students. None of the activities in this chapter take a lot of time: they can easily be integrated in your classes as you begin teaching required content during the first week of school. You might take 5 minutes at the beginning of class to let kids share a photo with a partner (see page 74), 15 minutes to ask students what they need from you (see page 69), or half a period to refine classroom norms (see page 88). By threading community-building work through your schedule, rather than lumping it all into a few of the first days of school, you show your students that they matter as individuals and that social skills are intertwined with academic success.

GOAL	MOVES
Build Relationships with Students	• Continue to Build Rapport with Your Students (page 64) • Mine Student Interest Surveys for Commonalities (page 67) • Ask Students, "What Do You Need from Me?" (page 69)
Build Relationships Among Students	• Help Kids Get to Know One Another Even Better (page 72) • Share Important Moments and Memories with Phone Photos (page 74) • Illustrate Student Interests with Sketchnote IDs (page 76)
Strengthen Classroom Norms	• Define Your Classroom as a Home Court (page 79) • Teach Collaborative Skills Directly (page 82) • Welcome New Students into the Community (page 85) • Have Students Promote the Class Norms (page 88) • Reinforce Friendliness and Support (page 92) • Put a Welcome Mat Out for Substitute Teachers (page 96)

Goal: Build Relationships with Students

Lessons to support this goal:

- Continue to Build Rapport with Your Students (page 64)

- Mine Student Interest Surveys for Commonalities (page 67)

- Ask Students, "What Do You Need from Me?" (page 69)

TRADITIONAL APPROACH	COLLABORATIVE APPROACH
• The teacher takes daily out-loud roll call. • The class has large-group discussions (including those in which the teacher cold-calls on students or otherwise polices contributions). • The teacher notices common interests with students haphazardly, as those interests become apparent to the teacher.	• The teacher systematically notes unique qualities about the students and engages students in brief positive conversations. • The teacher uses interest inventories to actively look for commonalities. • The teacher openly solicits student input about what best helps students learn.
⬇ LEADS TO ⬇	⬇ LEADS TO ⬇
∅ Roll call is a predictable and comfortable start to the period, but no rapport is generated with students. ∅ Verbose volunteers hold the floor in discussions while less engaged students tune out. ∅ The teacher bonds with some students while others remain a mystery, which can lead to student perceptions of (or actual) favoritism, bias, and discrimination.	✔ Students recognize that the teacher is really "seeing" them and is interested in them. This can lead to increased trust in the teacher. ✔ The teacher's recognition of commonalities with students enables the teacher to see them in a more positive way, which makes it more likely that the teacher can develop rapport with *all* students. ✔ Students feel seen and valued because the teacher asked for input—and then used it. This demonstrates to students that the teacher is flexible and sensitive to individual needs and will help all students thrive.

Figure 3.1

MOVE> Continue to Build Rapport with Your Students

Immediate Result: Students see that your interest in them is ongoing, not a "beginning of year" friendliness that starts to fizzle as the papers-to-grade pile grows and the press to cover content takes over.

Long-Term Result: As you continue to greet students at the door before class and bid them a good day when the bell rings, you have daily opportunities to get to know your students just a little bit better. Consequently, when the "honeymoon" period of the school year (about the first two weeks) fades and some inevitable tensions emerge, you and your students will already have some friendly investment in one another that will better enable you to solve problems together.

It is human nature to want to be noticed and recognized. Think about how you feel when a colleague engages you in a quick conversation about an interest of yours or when a supervisor offers you a quick appreciation of something positive she noticed as she walked by your classroom. Most likely, you feel that you are appreciated and that your presence in the school community does make a difference for others. This is the same way we want our students to feel as they walk into and out of our classrooms each and every day.

As we continue to voice specific "positive noticings" to our students, we concretely demonstrate our interest in them and our desire to see them at their best. These simple, momentary, brief interactions serve as the foundation that builds bridges and relationships that ultimately strengthen the classroom community and encourage students to make better behavior choices. The trick with these ongoing noticings is to remember your role. You are not trying to be a friend to your students; you are trying to be an adult who admires them and recognizes their potential as well as an adult whom they can rely on. What are some things you might want to keep in mind in these interactions?

- **Avoid oversharing or prying into personal relationships.** Though you might know a student has had a fight with their boyfriend, now is not the time to share stories of your past loves. Instead, you might just ask if there is anything you can do to help them feel better while they are in your class.

- **Avoid trying to imitate your students' talk styles.** Let them own their slang and their teen sarcasm. It's unlikely that imitating your students will make you "hip" in their eyes, and your attempts could be seen as insulting or appropriating. That said, you can compliment your students' talk styles and even ask them to be the language "experts" in that area, instructing you in their styles as a way to learn more about them and their world.

- **Keep in mind how your own identity might influence an interaction.** For example, depending on your gender identity and a student's gender identity, a well-intentioned compliment about the student's appearance might be misconstrued.

- **Catch students for a quick chat as they come into the room or in the last minutes of class.** Greet students at the door for quick conversations, and also roam the room the last minute or two as students are packing up. Your goal is to get your students talking about an interest of theirs, not yours (see Figure 3.2). Listening is a sign of your interest, while oversharing by the teacher whiffs of narcissism. Of course, it's all right to share some information about yourself if the student asks you a question and your answer is school appropriate.

Figure 3.2 **Samantha and her teacher established a rapport that included conversations about fashion and style.**

- **Offer noticings that are positive, affirming, and aspirational.** Also, as mentioned earlier, make these noticings specific and concrete. Don't tell a student they did a good job and leave it at that. Describe their good job in some detail! What might you say? Here are some examples:

- You really stood out as a leader in your group today when you _____, and that helped your partners dig deeper. Keep it up!

- I noticed you helping (student name) today when he was confused. Thank you!

- That question you shared in class today—_____—really made us think about (topic/content/text) in a new way. Thanks for sharing it!

- Your writing/annotation/discussion skills are really improving. I can tell you are working hard at it.

- I overheard when you said _____. I really love how you can work well with anyone in the class. That's a great life skill and makes our class a better place.

- You really got your group rolling into some deep conversation when you asked _____.

- I could tell you were dedicated to doing your best today when you _____.

- Thanks for sharing your excitement about what we did in class today.

- When you had the chance to work/write/read solo today, you were totally focused and used your time well.

An additional benefit to this practice is that it focuses *us* on noticing positive student behaviors, which in turn bolsters our resolve and compassion when a student makes a bad behavior choice. Since we've taken the effort to consciously and continually build relationships that help us get to know our students, when a student engages in a behavior that frustrates us (and they will because that is the nature of humans whether they are in fourth grade, in tenth grade, or adults), it will be much easier for us to see this as a momentary slipup, a problem that needs to be solved rather than a major personal affront or mean-spirited confrontation. Your personal inventory of positive interactions will prevent you from negatively defining a student based on an unfortunate gaff.

MOVE>Mine Student Interest Surveys for Commonalities

Immediate Result: Reviewing the interest surveys will give you personalized information and topics that you can use as you work to get to know and build rapport with your students.

Long-Term Result: Teasing out the commonalities you have with students will positively influence your attitude toward them: it's easier to see our students in multidimensional ways when we know we have things in common with them.

The interest surveys you used in the first days of school (see Chapter 2) provided some initial thinking on eventual interview topics as well as a little window into each student's world. Even better, these surveys can now provide you with an opportunity to find interests you have in common with your students.

You might think that finding these connections will be helpful to you in striking up conversations with students, which can build rapport and students' trust in you. However, a 2016 study published by the American Enterprise Institute gives us another, perhaps even more powerful, reason to find commonalities with your students: those commonalities affect *our* perceptions of our students. The researchers report:

> *Teachers who learned that they shared commonalities with their students . . . rated their relationships with those students more positively. In contrast, students who learned they shared commonalities with their teacher did not significantly alter their perceptions of their relationship with the teacher. When teachers learned about commonalities, students garnered higher grades in that teacher's class. (Gehlbach and Robinson 2016)*

From this study, I think we can take a cue. When you collect those interest surveys, read through them and jot some notes for yourself (see Figure 3.3). Look for

Background/Interest Survey

Name _____

Date _____ Hour _____

1. Places you've lived

2. Pets you've had or would like to have   Huskys – We had a Malamute once – they are like huskies

3. Favorite music artist/group/song   Lil Pump

4. Good vacation spots that you've visited or would like to visit   Kalihari – I like the surfing there! (It is about all I could handle – I could never do real surfing!)

5. Out of school pursuits/hobbies   Fishing / Playing Bball

6. Favorite subject other than this class!   None

7. Languages you speak or would like to learn   Fluent English

8. Favorite foods   Steak ♡

9. Favorite television shows   Storage Wars

10. Favorite zoo animal   Tiger

11. Favorite holiday   Christmas ♡

12. Household chores: Which ones are okay, which ones do you hate?   hate all   scoop poop, walk dog   dishes, putting ~~toys~~ clothes away   I am with you!

Figure 3.3 **When students walk into class, Cindi offers personalized greetings with these topics in mind.**

commonalities. Equally important: pick out items that students can educate you on as you make some personal connections with each student. Then, every day, pick out a couple of kids you're going to talk up each period. Based on the survey, you might start the conversation like this: "Hey, I saw that you put down _____ as your favorite music artist. I don't know his work. If I were to watch just one of his videos on YouTube, which one would you recommend? Why that one?" If you don't think you're going to remember the name of the song, have the student write it down for you. And, most important, take 5 minutes to get on YouTube and watch that video so that the next time you catch that student for a quick conversation, you can talk about it.

Reviewing your notes from those interest surveys will give you openings for some personalized doorway conversations. Even though the initial research showed that letting students know you had common interests didn't seem to affect *them* in a measurable sense, the more *you* talk with students about their interests as well as your shared interests, the better *you* will perceive your students, which in turn is likely to bring out their best!

MOVE> Ask Students, "What Do You Need from Me?"

Immediate Result: Students get an immediate opportunity to advise you on how they hope the class will operate and how to respond to their learning needs.

Long-Term Result: These beginning-of-year suggestions become a touchstone for your own reflection as you plan. Actively referencing and using students' advice builds trust. As students become more comfortable with you and their classmates, this topic can be revisited periodically. Most likely, later answers will demonstrate greater depth and insight because of the trust that has developed.

While the emphasis on class norms is typically focused on shaping student behavior, holding ourselves to the same standard shows students that we take the work of building a fair and friendly classroom seriously.

Early in the year, Mississippi seventh-grade teacher Lindsey Jones asks her students, "What do you need from me so that you can do your best learning this year?" She gives each student a sticky note and a few minutes to think and write. Sometimes students ask if they can make more than one suggestion. Lindsey answers by asking how many more sticky notes they need. Once the sticky notes are ready, she invites a row or two at a time to step up and add their stickies to a chart (see Figure 3.4).

What kinds of things do kids write?

- To just encourage us because that makes us do better

- Feedback

- Be helpful, understanding, and motivating

- Inspirational

Figure 3.4 **Seventh-grade boys add their sticky-note suggestions as well as read what others have written.**

- Caring

- Joyful

- Respectful

- Fun

These suggestions are nothing surprising, nothing earth-shattering, and nothing you probably aren't already trying to do. Yet actually asking students for their input recognizes students as individuals, amplifies their voices, and makes them feel totally different than when someone just assumes they know what they need. After all notes are posted, Lindsey moves the poster to her workstation, where she can reflect on her students' needs and desires and request further clarification when needed as she plans her lessons (see Figure 3.5).

Figure 3.5 Lindsey posts her seventh-grade students' suggestions on the wall where she does most of her lesson planning, which offers her a quick opportunity to cross-check her intended instruction with what students need in order to learn best.

As the year progresses, maybe once a quarter, revisit the chart with students. After working with you and one another, they've probably had certain concerns met while other issues might have arisen. Ask students to visit the chart and remove the sticky notes they originally wrote. Then pass out some new sticky notes. Ask, "Now that we are well into the school year, what do you need from me so that you can continue to do your best learning? If you want to repost your ideas from the beginning of the year, that's fine. If you have some different ideas you'd like to share now, write them down on the sticky notes. If you'd like to repost some of your original suggestions as well as some new ideas, that's fine as well." And then, once the suggestions are revised, continue to use your students' ideas as you plan.

Goal: Build Relationships Among Students

Lessons to support this goal:

- Help Kids Get to Know One Another Even Better (page 72)

- Share Important Moments and Memories with Phone Photos (page 74)

- Illustrate Student Interests with Sketchnote IDs (page 76)

TRADITIONAL APPROACH	COLLABORATIVE APPROACH
• The class focuses heavily on icebreaking at the beginning of the year. • Community-building attempts are forgotten as content coverage takes center stage.	• Structured opportunities for icebreaking and new acquaintanceship occur on a near-daily basis. • Opportunities are given for students to share in various modalities. • Interviewing skills are explicitly demonstrated and honed.
⬇ LEADS TO ⬇	⬇ LEADS TO ⬇
Ø Students become disconnected from those they do not know well. Ø Cliques reemerge. Ø Skills necessary for small-group collaboration and discussion go unpracticed. Ø Lack of connection between students and between the teacher and students means that disruptions can easily turn into confrontations or lead students to shut down.	✔ Students expand acquaintanceship, developing friendships and working relationships with many classmates. ✔ Frequent low-stakes interviewing refines listening and follow-up questioning skills, which are essential for student-led discussion. ✔ Opportunities for sharing interests enable the teacher to learn more about the students. ✔ Disruptions can more often be settled productively because there are strong foundational relationships in place between students and between the teacher and students.

Figure 3.6

MOVE>Help Kids Get to Know One Another Even Better

Immediate Result: Students continue to hone their interviewing skills as they become acquainted with class members they might not have talked to on their own.

Long-Term Result: As students get to know one another, they are far more likely to treat one another with respect. Plus, the skills practiced while interviewing—asking good questions based on careful listening—are the foundation skills for any small-group academic discussion.

The peer interviews your students did on the first day of school about fun but low-risk topics (see Help Kids Get to Know You and One Another Through Interviewing, page 49) can be even more powerful when you make them a part of how you begin class each day. In the 5 minutes while students are interviewing each other, you can take attendance, pass back papers, and complete any other housekeeping chores that arise at the beginning of class.

At first, pull topics from that first-day interest survey since students have already had a chance to think about them. As first described in Chapter 2, continue to give students the opportunity to interview you. Your modeling the role of the interview subject gives students guided practice in careful listening and asking open-ended follow-up questions that dig deeper into the topic, thus revealing greater details and insight from the interview subject.

Frequent interviewing enables students to comfortably begin to expand their acquaintanceships with those they don't know. Once students have repeatedly interviewed their nearby seatmates (those they sit next to and across from) and gotten to know them (this will require two to three weeks of daily interviewing), congratulate the class on their improved interviewing skills. Then tell them the reward for their skillfulness is a new seat and some new interview partners: the goal is for each student to get to know and work with every classmate by the end of the semester or year. When an absence creates one student without a partner (two students with missing partners can team up), chuck your housekeeping and be that student's interview partner. This gives you the opportunity to model interviewing one-on-one, give one student your undivided attention, learn something about them, and maybe give that student a new insight into you.

This work goes a long way toward creating a class where students treat one another well: it is much easier to be mean to strangers than to those with whom you have relationships. Additionally, in conversation, we tend to be more interested in the ideas of people we know than in those of strangers, and being interested in the ideas of group members during an academic discussion completely determines the depth of thinking that will take place (see Figures 3.7 and 3.8).

Figure 3.7 **As these sophomores become practiced interviewers, they can begin making their own lists of potential (and school-appropriate) interview topics and then choose from them when it is time to interview each other.**

Figure 3.8 **These fourth-grade boys have each created a list of topics they'd enjoy being interviewed on. When they trade, their partner chooses a topic he finds intriguing.**

MOVE>Share Important Moments and Memories with Phone Photos

Immediate Result: Students see that you appreciate that smartphones are part of their culture. Plus, students get to share something that matters to them.

Long-Term Result: This activity helps students get to know about one another's lives beyond school, helping them deepen their connections. There are academic benefits, as well: when this activity is repeated, students get better and better at picking out important details when they choose a photo to share and when they look at others' photos, the same skill necessary when studying visual content (or, really, any content).

There are two things we all have in common these days:

> We can't keep our hands off our smartphones.

> We all love to take pictures with our phones.

Ask your class, "How many of you have a slew of photos on your phone?" Probably almost everyone will raise a hand. Then continue:

> *Me, too. Since taking photos with our phones is such a part of all of our lives these days, let's try using these photos to learn more about each other. I'm going to give you a minute to get your phones out and open up your photo album. Choose a photo or photos that tell a story or revive an important memory that your partner could interview you on—and that are appropriate for school.*
>
> *If you don't have your phone with you, that's okay—just think about one or two things that happened to you recently. Just as with the photos, they might be something really amazing, or they might be just a fun time you had hanging out with friends or something really cute your baby nephew did. To give other people enough details to really "see" the situation, you'll need to describe things a bit— what details can you include about what it looked like?*

Model by projecting some of your own phone photos for the class to see. Explain what they are looking at. For example, I might say, "Here's a photo of some Venus flytraps I saw at an indoor garden in Grand Rapids, Michigan. I love Venus flytraps! And this was only one of the carnivorous plant species on display" (see Figure 3.9). Then let students interview you, asking their best open-ended questions so that they can find out why you find the photo(s) interesting and what memories are attached. Then turn the kids back to their partners to talk about and be interviewed about their photos as you eavesdrop, view, and maybe photobomb a few selfies (see Figures 3.10).

Figure 3.9 **Sharing photos gives us a way into conversation.**

Figure 3.10 **Students are thrilled when a teacher tells them to get their phones out; everyone has photos they can't wait to share and be interviewed on!**

MOVE> Illustrate Student Interests with Sketchnote IDs

Immediate Result: Sketchnote IDs offer yet another avenue for your students to get to know one another. Anything students draw is fine, and for those who are reluctant to think in doodles and images, this activity gives them a safe way to experiment with this form of communication.

Long-Term Result: The kinds of conversations that sketchnote IDs spark support a genuinely collaborative classroom. Sketchnote IDs also serve as another personal interest inventory that might offer ideas for students as they look for writing or inquiry inspiration. Finally, as students become familiar and comfortable with sketchnoting, this visual organization technique can be applied to most academic note-taking tasks.

Dan Weinstein, an English teacher at Great Neck South High School on Long Island, aims to have his students think creatively and visually early in the school year as they create student IDs that rely on a combination of words, images, and vivid color. Dan begins by handing out extra-large (5-×-8-inch) index cards, explaining, "The idea here is for you to mind map your passions, activities, hobbies, and anything else that you really love." Dan shows students numerous examples from previous students, encourages them to get started, and gives them workshop time for some first-draft brainstorming and sketching in their notebooks before they commit to a final draft on the note card. Dan asks students to submit their final versions, which are often quite highly designed, a few days later (see Figures 3.11, 3.12, and 3.13). Here's how Dan concludes this assignment:

> *When my students all have their ID cards ready, I lead them in a whip around the room. Each and every student explains a bit about the topics on their cards,*

Figure 3.11 In his sketchnote ID, Connor decided to focus on four aspects of his life: social media, sports, food, and Netflix.

Figure 3.12 Gianna's sketchnote ID organizes her ideas in a different way. She displays many interests and favorites; some are explained with words and images, while others are represented with image alone.

Figure 3.13 Sketchnote IDs nurture a natural curiosity in one's classmates because the images grab attention and make a viewer want to start asking questions. The details in the IDs offer numerous openings for student interviewing (discussed in Help Kids Get to Know One Another Even Better earlier in this chapter).

which almost always display effort and wonderful art from nonartists. Then students move into smaller groups to talk about their interests in more detail.

I hold these index cards in my hands in class during the first few weeks of school and use them to get to know the students. Once I have the names memorized, I turn them into a bulletin board that looks awesome and inspires many compliments. In the spring, students add them to their portfolios.

Goal: Strengthen Classroom Norms

Lessons to support this goal:

TRADITIONAL APPROACH	COLLABORATIVE APPROACH
• Behavior rules are written by the teacher or administration and are typically included in the beginning-of-year syllabus. • Students are told how to behave. Rules are developed without any student input.	• The teacher and students work together to explicitly define positive interaction skills. • The behavior list is a living document. Problems are discussed and norms are revised as needed. • Interpersonal skills are explicitly demonstrated and honed.
⬇ LEADS TO ⬇	⬇ LEADS TO ⬇
Ø Rules are mostly forgotten by students until the teacher must enforce them. The teacher may feel frustrated and isolated when enforcing the rules. Ø From the students' perspective, rules may seem to benefit only the teacher. Ø Teacher-imposed rules do not encourage student ownership, student behavior reflection, or refinement. Ø How students react to newcomers is unpredictable; reactions are based on students' personalities rather than community behavior values.	✔ Students are invested in the norms, remembering and reminding one another of behavior expectations as they work together. ✔ Polite, friendly, helpful behavior creates an inclusive environment for all students. ✔ Students see their interaction skills improve, and content talk becomes more accountable. ✔ Students and teachers enjoy one another's company and celebrate their classroom accomplishments. ✔ New students and substitute teachers are welcomed into the community.

Figure 3.14

MOVE>Define Your Classroom as a Home Court

> **Immediate Result:** Students identify actions and behaviors that will support a collaborative classroom.
>
> **Long-Term Result:** Students internalize supportive behaviors, helping one another thrive, and recognize that there is no need for competition between class members. Students share in the responsibility of keeping the tone of the classroom friendly and supportive. Students have an increased sense of safety in the classroom and are more comfortable taking social and academic risks.

Given the snarky comments and name-calling so evident on social media, I bet you've noticed that many students are skillful in the "art of the put-down." Popular and enduring sitcoms such as *The Simpsons* or *The Big Bang Theory* also lean heavily on the comic use of the put-down within their scripts. And of course, fictional characters can put each other down episode after episode and still remain friends, unless a particularly hurtful comment leads to some intended drama that is still neatly wrapped up within the episode. However, in real life people do not bounce right back after having a good laugh with the person who launched the put-down. The risk of being the victim of a put-down quickly establishes a classroom atmosphere of unease, mistrust, and fear. And under these conditions, students are highly unlikely to share opinions, take educational risks, or even be able to fully concentrate on the content. All it takes is one sarcastic, humiliating comment to completely shut down a student. How logically and rationally can you think when you are angry or upset? When these negative emotions have taken center stage, the brain goes into survival mode—flight or fight—which makes it impossible for learning to occur. If we want a collaborative classroom, everyone in the class needs to avoid put-downs.

To open up the conversation with students, you might just ask them about their own favorite sitcoms, encouraging them to share why the shows are funny. Pretty soon, students will begin to notice that most of these shows find their comedy in sarcasm, put-downs, and delighting in the misfortune of other characters. After this realization, move the discussion to how people in real life respond to a consistent barrage of put-downs and lack of support. You might say:

> *It's scientifically proven that when people feel hurt or angry—the way they typically feel after an insult—their brains cannot make good decisions or learn well. That's why when you get in an argument with someone you never say the right thing. Your brain is too agitated with negative emotions to respond in a logical, calm way. Knowing all that, we can see that it's super important that everyone feel calm and safe in class.*
>
> *So we're going to use an analogy that will help all of us remember to treat each other in ways that will help make all of us successful. That analogy is home court. Did you know that many teams, particularly school and amateur, win more games at home than when they are away [LaMeres 1990]? This used to also apply consistently to professional sports until teams began using elite training resources such as sports, psychologists, sleep coaches, and "virtual-technology training [that lets] athletes act out the scenarios they might encounter" (Schonbrun 2020). Why do you think teams might win more games at home? Work with your partner to make a list of all the reasons [see Figure 3.15].*

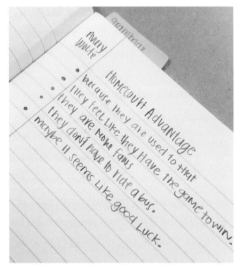

Figure 3.15 **Though reasons listed for the home court advantage will vary among partners, almost all pairs will consistently list the importance of fan support and environmental predictability.**

After a first brainstorm, have students return to their lists and prioritize the items according to how much they believe each reason actually affects a team. To create an idea summary, pairs can take turns reading an idea to the class. Give the students these instructions:

> *When it is your turn, read your number one idea. If that has already been mentioned, read your number two, and so on. If all your ideas have been presented, go back to your number one and read that.*

Write students' responses on the board as they share them, adding checks to any responses you hear more than once. Then ask:

How do fan support and a comfortable playing field relate to the academic success of the people in this room? How can we create a home court advantage here?

Pass out index cards and give students a couple of minutes to write their ideas and share with a partner. Let volunteers share ideas or collect the cards and read some of the responses aloud. Record each shared idea on a class anchor chart. If students do not name the idea of avoiding insults, add it to the list, explaining why it is essential in establishing a collaborative community. Then explain how the entire class will be responsible for this community:

From now on, this room is our home court. We are each other's teammates as well as each other's fans. As teammates and fans, we want to see all of us succeed. From now on, our role is to treat each other with respect and support and avoid insults and put-downs.

"Home court" might sound like a pretty simple idea, but I've seen it work in elementary schools, middle schools, and high schools and with groups of adults. Since teen brain physiology desires safety, students breathe a sigh of relief during and after this activity because it immediately establishes a norm that insults and put-downs are unacceptable. This safety then enables students to comfortably share their ideas in class discussion because they don't have to worry about others voicing negative judgment. Interestingly, once students understand the concept of home court, they have a heightened awareness of the hurtful nature of humor at the expense of others, thus extinguishing much of this negative behavior right at the beginning of the school year. You may even find, as I did with my own classes, that students shout, "Home court!" as a celebratory reminder to others to keep this space safe.

See Reinforce Friendliness and Support later in this chapter to help students take the home court advantage to heart.

MOVE> Teach Collaborative Skills Directly

Immediate Result: Students try out collaborative skills in the classroom.

Long-Term Result: Positive collaborative skills become integrated into students' behaviors as they work together, heightening student awareness as they interact with other students in academic tasks and decreasing the likelihood of conflicts.

The class norm companion of home court is the baseline skill of being friendly and supportive. No deep learning, student engagement and collaboration, or teacher satisfaction can exist unless those in that classroom treat one another well. However, lots of us make the big mistake of assuming students automatically know how to interact in order to get the best out of one another. If every one of your students had mastered this skill, then we wouldn't even have to talk about shaping positive classroom norms, right? But the fact that we are having this discussion means that we need to be clear about what helpful behaviors look like in the classroom—in life, for that matter. We must teach soft skills just as explicitly as we teach our content: it is those very soft skills that will affect how well students learn and remember our content.

The first step in teaching these skills—or *any* skills—is to define them and show their importance, their real-life value.

Ask your students to silently take a moment to consider a time when someone else was friendly and supportive to them, focusing on the details of what the person said or did. Then have pairs discuss what someone would do if they were treating another with friendliness and support. What would their facial expressions, body language, gestures, and posture look like? And what would people actually say to one another if they were being friendly and supportive? What would it sound like?

Looks Like	Sounds Like

Figure 3.16 **A T-chart is a clear and expedient way of working with your students to define an important collaborative or academic skill so that students truly understand what they need to do and say. You will see this chart referred to and used throughout the book.**

Have each set of student partners fold one sheet of paper in half lengthwise to create a "Looks Like" and "Sounds Like" T-chart (see Figure 3.16 and Online Resource 3.1) and to brainstorm and jot answers to the questions just posed. If pairs are stumped, give an example for each column such as "smiling" for "Looks Like" and "Hi, how are you today?" for "Sounds Like."

While pairs work, pass back the "How Would You Like to Be Remembered?" cards (see Chapter 2, page 46) from the first day and tell pairs to see if they can add more ideas based on what they were thinking that day. As the brainstorming concludes, bring the class back around to complete a master list. Try to get a response from each pair (either column is fine) so that everyone gets an idea on the chart. Remember, though, that some pairs will have more ideas than others, and this activity will be harder for students who have not done much thinking about skills before. Be patient. If a student comes up with a negatively phrased suggestion such as "No one says 'shut up,'" ask the partners how they came up with that. Maybe they were thinking that everyone's ideas would be considered. Then ask how the negative statement could be turned into a positive one, such as "Let's get everyone's opinions before we decide."

When the students have finished working, post their charts in the classroom. Creating the charts is a good exercise, but it's how we *use* the charts going forward that really matters. Make the skills on the charts prerequisites for small-group discussions: when students get together, remind them that you want to see them and hear them using friendliness and support. And then monitor the groups for that skill. Even if a group is on task, intervene for a minute if they are forgetting to demonstrate their friendliness and support skills, saying:

> I see you are having a great discussion and I like the way you are on task! Now let's take a friendliness and support break. First, each of you say something friendly and supportive to your group. You can read something off the chart or you can invent a new positive phrase right now.

Let members each take a turn. Then continue:

> I'm going to move on to another group in a second, but before I go I want you to look at the chart again. What's a "Looks Like" item each of you could start doing as you return to your discussions? Tell me know what you're going to start doing as soon as you jump back into your conversation.

Figure 3.17 Andrea Arndt's seventh-grade class created this friendliness and support chart.

Listen to the goals, noticing and affirming as appropriate. Your friendliness and support matters, too!

Any skill-defining T-chart is always a work in progress. As students work together and practice being friendly and supportive to one another, it's important to return to the chart frequently to add additional examples and define some initially vague descriptors in more specific terms. Also, items on an initial chart might offer fodder for some new charts. For example, on the chart in Figure 3.17, it might be worth taking the time to create new charts for the skills "being kind" and "helping new students."

MOVE>Welcome New Students into the Community

Immediate Result: On the day you do this work with your students, the class will have an opportunity to consider how the class is a community. Additionally, when a new student appears in your classroom, your students will be able to take on some of the day-disrupting tasks of getting them acclimated.

Long-Term Result: The new student will soon feel at home in the classroom community, and the addition of the new student will not disrupt the class community you've been building together. Students will also see how to become more sensitive, empathetic, and helpful to newcomers in settings beyond the classroom.

An almost iron-clad guarantee for most teachers is that sometime during the school year at least one new student will appear without prior warning. Trying to bring a new student up to speed when everyone else is in the swing of the semester is a challenge for teachers, but just imagine how that new students feels. Here they are in a new setting, plunged into unfamiliar classes. And students who are new to the school (not just to your class) may still be trying to just navigate the physical building and make sense of a school culture that might be very different from the previous one—all without the benefit of established friendships or even familiar faces. Also, families do not generally pull children up by the roots and transfer them to a new school unless it is absolutely necessary, so besides the stress of entering a new school, a transfer student might also be dealing with outside considerations that compound this stress. So, as teachers and students, what can we do? Plan for how to embrace new students far before one ever turns up.

A good way to start is to ask students to discuss times when they have been new to a situation. You might start by having students write about those experiences for a couple of minutes and then move to partner interviews (see page 49) so that they have the chance to talk, share, and clarify their experiences.

Next, using the experiences they just discussed, have pairs make a list of the possible positives and negatives of being a transfer student. Allow pairs to talk and write for a few minutes, and then consolidate everyone's ideas into a class list. Students might suggest items such as

Positives	Negatives
Make new friends	Don't know anyone
Fresh start	Don't know your way around the school
People are interested in you	No one to sit with at lunch
	Don't know the school's culture
	Might be behind in some classes
	Nervous, afraid you'll make a mistake
	Afraid of bullying

More than likely, students will come up with more negatives than positives just because there really are a lot of negative feelings and circumstances when one is thrown into a completely new environment with little prior preparation. Plus, sometimes students get a (misguided) sense of power from being mean to newcomers and excluding them. If you sense students might struggle with this issue, an excellent book to read aloud and discuss is *Each Kindness* by Jacqueline Woodson, a picture book that works just as well with adults, high school students, and middle school students as it does with younger children. Told from the perspective of a girl who actively excludes and subtly bullies a new student, the story demonstrates that this behavior hurts the new student while offering nothing positive to the main character. It shows how the narrator is left with the realization that she contributed to irreparable harm and can never make amends because the new student disappears as suddenly as she arrives.

Segue from this "new student" discussion to using the "Looks Like"/"Sounds Like" T-chart strategy from the previous move Teach Collaborative Skills Directly. This time the T-chart will define how we can best treat newcomers in our classroom. Ask students, "If we were to get a new student in our class, how would we want to act, and what would we want to say that would make them feel welcome and comfortable? Since being a newcomer can offer some unpleasant consequences, let's focus on a T-chart that will remind us how to behave and keep that from happening."

MAKING OTHERS FEEL WELCOME IN OUR CLASSROOM

Looks Like	Sounds Like
Smiling	"How's it going? Need any advice?"
Friendly	"I'll be your partner."
Attentive posture	"When do you have lunch?"
Enthusiastic partner work	"Come with me. I'll introduce you to my friends."

Post the T-chart after its creation, noting that it's not just new students who require us to use the skill of welcoming. During the course of the year, the class will probably also encounter observing administrators and colleagues, substitute teachers, or even a student teacher.

The final preparation step is to ask the class for a few students who are willing to be ambassadors. These are students whose job it will be to help a new student make a smooth transition into the class and, if possible, to also give a hand elsewhere within the school day if a new student might need it. Also, ask for some volunteers who are willing to move to another seat without hesitation if the class has to make a quick rearrangement to accommodate a new student and their ambassador.

And then it's time to wait for the new-student moment (see Figure 3.18). When your new student does appear without warning, point to the welcoming T-chart, greet that student warmly, and introduce them to their ambassador. Of course, also arrange for time when you can talk with them privately to understand their background and help accommodate their academic and social–emotional needs. And, as you continue community-building work throughout the year, your new student will have more opportunities to build connections with peers and with you.

Figure 3.18 **Eighth graders participating in an up-and-moving mingle with the goal of meeting those they don't know well (including some recently arrived students).**

MOVE>Have Students Promote the Class Norms

> **Immediate Result:** Students identify class norms.
>
> **Long-Term Result:** The posters that students make become constant reminders of positive and intentional behavior expectations. Also, if a student accidentally slips up and says something unkind, the quickest way to get back on track is to point toward the posters on the wall and ask, "What's something you can say right now that expresses friendliness and support?"

Believe it or not, between the moves of Home Court (page 79) and Friendliness and Support (page 92), your class has already negotiated a positive operating agreement. When your students defined these concepts in their own words, they constructed these norms:

- Be sensitive and empathetic to the feelings of others.
- Help others when needed.
- Support one another so that all can be successful.
- Come prepared for class.
- Behave in ways that will help one another learn.

The result? You don't have to give the students rules. They've already written them. Not only is this list likely very similar to the rules you'd have named, but it's also likely to be more effective than rules you announce by decree. When students negotiate expectations themselves, they're more invested in them and more willing to internalize them.

If you are reluctant to give up your rules, remember that we teachers tend to get a bit overzealous in our rule making because we can imagine every worst-case scenario thanks to our years in the classroom. But the more rules we try to enforce, the less likely our students will remember any of them. When it comes to rules, keep it simple. Add and define a new norm with students when the need arises. As students continue to work together, other behaviors will eventually need to be defined, such as including everyone, equally participating in a conversation, or backing up one's opinion with text. But these are conversation refinements and fine-tuning that will only become necessary once students treat one another in friendly, respectful, supportive ways whenever they work together.

Now it is time to name the class' baseline rules publicly. Tell the class:

> *Even though we have established home court and defined what friendliness and support look like and sound like, it still takes some effort to remember this whenever we work together. So, with your partner, we're going to make some reminder posters. If you're on this side of the room, you will create posters advertising home court. Those of you on that side of the room will create posters advertising friendliness and support. Now I want one partner from each pair to get some supplies.*

Have pencils, erasers, markers, and paper out. If you have chart paper available, you can cut sheets in half. Then continue with your instructions:

> *Imagine that your poster is a mini-billboard. Its goal is to attract and educate viewers. Also, a good billboard makes strong use of key words as well as visuals that help the viewer understand and remember. Since this poster is a product of both partners, begin by situating the paper and your desks and chairs so that both of you can work on it at the same time [see Figure 3.19]. Before you start making marks on your poster, review your notes and our anchor charts for home court and friendliness and support and think about how you could represent these ideas more visually, using mainly images and a few words as well. Sketch your poster out and double-check the spelling on any words you're using before you start coloring with the markers. If you have any questions, I'll be cruising around the room and checking in as you work. Stay focused! The posters have to be done by the end of today's class.*

Figure 3.19 **Notice how these partners have arranged their poster sheet between them so that both can work on it at the same time.**

Be sure to have a blank wall ready to receive all the posters from all your classes (see Figure 3.20). Once they are posted, let your class study the artwork and the messages. Then say, "This is a fantastic representation of the ways we want to act and treat each other in this classroom. It's something we need to look at and remember every day we work together."

Letting students see their own words and work as the rules of the class is more powerful than providing students with your own list of rules or prodding them through the process of working with you to create a detailed list of teacher-approved rules for the year. However, if you're looking for a quick way to sum up students' ideas, Health Sciences High School and Middle College uses a succinct list to remind students of their expected norms (Frey, Fisher, and Smith 2019, 92):

> Take care of yourself.
>
> Take care of each other.
>
> Take care of this place.

Figure 3.20 Though you might be reluctant to devote an entire wall to these posters, it is totally worth it: their continual presence sets a collaborative and appreciative tone for the rest of the year. Plus, if you get them up before back-to-school night, you will be surprised at the positive feedback you will receive from parents and guardians who are delighted that their children (especially their *teenage* children) are in a classroom where friendly, supportive, and respectful behaviors are clearly defined and reinforced.

Once the posters are up in your classroom, it's helpful for students to consider how they might condense the various messages into their own three rules. Even though the posters are up and the kids understand these skills, the challenging part is getting the kids to actively demonstrate home court and friendliness and support as they work with others. Using a new skill requires new thinking and new behaviors; it is much easier to just act the same way and say the same things you always have.

In the beginning, students will need to be reminded of "the rules" every time they work together; following the rules means pairs are displaying positive body language, actively using friendly and supportive language, and treating the room as home court. As students team up for work, teacher monitoring is very important. Walk around, listening in as pairs work together. Compliment and encourage when pairs are friendly and supportive. If you need to intervene when students are neglecting friendliness and support, you might say:

> *Today is the day I am really looking for everyone to use lots of friendly and supportive statements with each other. When I came to your group, I wasn't hearing much, so I want you to stop your discussion for a moment and practice together. Think of something positive you can say to your group/partner right now. Take a look at our poster wall and grab an idea. Now let's hear something from each member. [When students conclude, remind them to keep their positivity roll going.]*

You'll find more suggestions about how to support students in upholding these norms in Reinforce Friendliness and Support—the next move in this chapter.

MOVE>Reinforce Friendliness and Support

Immediate Result: Students maintain behavior that makes teaching and learning possible each day.

Long-Term Result: Students feel safe in class and their behavior and academic progress are not hampered by worry or anger. Students have daily opportunities to be supportive of others and to work collaboratively, skills that will serve them well in school and in the workplace.

When students are learning to make friendliness and support part of their academic lives in class, their attempts may look or sound forced when you're standing right there and insisting, but isn't every conscious behavior change awkward at first? Why would using a new skill be any different? Kids may have ways of being friendly and supportive with friends or family, but putting these skills to use in a classroom may be a new challenge for them. Expect that as students learn to use a new skill they will move through very predictable steps: reluctance, awkwardness, overuse, and integration (see Chapter 2, page 53, for more about these steps).

Just as writing the classroom norms was a collaborative effort between you and your students, integrating them should also be a collaborative effort. The trick with nurturing the use of a new skill is to keep momentum. At first, we are keen monitors, reminding students to use a new skill in their collaborative work, but several weeks later that skill can be forgotten as we move on to the next curricular item. It's up to us to keep home court and friendliness and support at the forefront. As students become more adept and comfortable in their use of friendliness and support, the skill transforms from "that thing our teacher makes us do" to a true celebration.

Here are a few ideas for coaching students to use the skills in this chapter often and well:

- Review the friendliness and support anchor chart before a discussion and have each student write down three "Sounds Like" statements to use that day. Afterward, have each student think of one new statement to add to the chart.

- During monitoring, write down the skill observations you see or hear or keep tally (see Figures 3.21 and 3.22). What might you hear and jot down?

  - "Good job."
  - "Casey, you go next."
  - "Thank you."
  - "Good eye contact, group focus, and smiling."

Friendliness and Support Tally

DISCUSSION 1

Group 1	Group 2	Group 3	Group 4	Group 5	TOTAL
III	III	III	III	IIII	16

DISCUSSION 2

Group 1	Group 2	Group 3	Group 4	Group 5	TOTAL
THL	IIII	THL I	III	THL III	26

DISCUSSION 3

Group 1	Group 2	Group 3	Group 4	Group 5	TOTAL
THL III	THL	THL II	THL	THL IIII	34

Figure 3.21 As you observe groups, keep a tally of each time you hear a friendliness and support phrase. Give the class a total and make an improvement goal for next time: "Let's see if you can break twenty in our second discussion!"

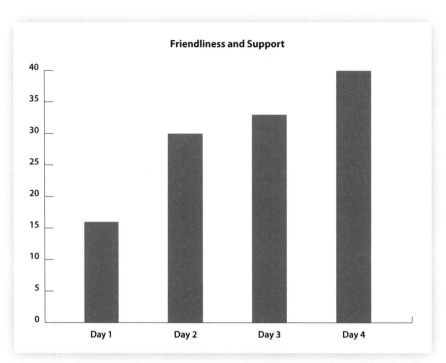

Friendliness and Support

Figure 3.22 **Graph ongoing results and post them for the class to see. Discuss the data with students: What trends do they see? How do they account for any dips in their use of the skills? How can they better use friendliness and support skills?**

In truth, anything that students are doing that shows inclusivity and their appreciation of one another's efforts is worth writing down. Once you have your notes, you can intervene in a group briefly to give your positive report. And later, once the class has reconvened, mention something positive each group did as you observed them during the day's small-group discussions.

- Have students name situations beyond your class where friendliness and support could be used. Then challenge students to go out, use the skill, and then report back to class on what effect it had on the group interaction. I'll never forget the time a student told me about how he used his friendliness and support skills when he was meeting his girlfriend's father for the first time. The father liked him!

- As you observe, use sticky notes to jot down the positive things you noticed, and give them to the kids you observed.

- Review the skill as a class. Talk about problems in usage and where refinement has taken place. You might say:

  In your groups, take a moment and think about when you most use the skill of friendliness and support. Is at the beginning, in the middle, or toward the end of your discussion? Now, think about when you use it the least. What can your group do to remember to use this skill at those times you are least likely to use it? What ideas can you share with the rest of us?

- Review and revise the original friendliness and support T-chart, adding new "Sounds Like" phrases and "Looks Like" descriptors that students have been using. You might say:

  Now that we've been working on using friendliness and support for a few weeks, what are some new "Looks Like" and "Sounds Like" phrases we can add to the chart? Take a couple of minutes to brainstorm ideas in your group and then we'll add the new ideas to our current lists.

  I've seen students come up with ideas such as

  - Appoint one member to remind us.

  - Make signs we can hold up that say "Friendliness and Support" whenever one of us decides we need to take a skill time-out.

  - Assign one person to this skill, but when that person gives us a friendliness and support phrase, the rest of us each have to say one as well.

MOVE>Put a Welcome Mat Out for Substitute Teachers

Immediate Result: Students feel invested in their time with the substitute teacher because *they* helped make the plans. The sub gets a clear set of plans and (we hope) a cooperative class.

Long-Term Result: Students see the class as something that they are responsible for. Students see a substitute as a guest, often unfamiliar with the particulars of the classroom, who therefore must be treated with patience and helpfulness.

Figure 3.23 David Finkle is an honest-to-goodness middle school and high school English teacher and a cartoonist. His strips are based on his own classroom experiences. You can check out all his comics at http://www.mrfitz.com.

Plan Together

The best way to change our students' perception of a "sub day" (see Figure 3.23) is for you and the class to plan together.

Early in the year, work with your students to create a plan that would work for everyone in the case of an emergency, an occasion when you are called away on such short notice you wouldn't have time to figure anything out. Discuss the typical activities that occur with regularity in your class, and determine what would work best in case you are suddenly absent. Remind students that the goal is not a "free day," but a day that moves learning forward. Don't be surprised if different classes come up with different plans. As long as the plans are feasible and academically sound, go with the classes' suggestions. Once the plans are finalized, stash a copy of the plans where an emergency sub can find them, but also give a copy to your school's substitute coordinator.

If you're making plans for a planned absence, don't keep your lesson plans a secret: share them with the class and hammer out the final details together. Also, whenever possible, do your best to have the class continue on as if you were there rather than default to a superfluous textbook assignment or watching a movie. Be up front with your students: tell them just because you're not going to be there doesn't mean that learning has to grind to a halt. Once plans are finalized, type them up and distribute hard copies or electronic copies to both students and the sub.

Next, use the now-familiar-to-students "Looks Like"/"Sounds Like" strategy to discuss what kinds of behavior will be helpful and productive when they are working with the substitute. A co-created class T-chart might look like Figure 3.24. Finally, ask for two or three volunteers to be "sub helpers" when you're absent. In my experience, almost without fail, the kids who are most likely to misbehave will be the same ones who

WORKING SUCCESSFULLY WITH A SUBSTITUTE TEACHER	
Looks Like	**Sounds Like**
• Sitting in the correct seat	• Silent individual work
• Giving substitute full attention	• Low-voiced group work
• Following directions	• "Hi _____, how are you today?"
• Staying seated	• "Is there anything you need help with?"
• Being friendly and helpful	• "Come sit down in our group and listen to what we've written."
• Focused on the academic task	• Giving information or advice to the substitute when asked
• Patient and understanding	

Figure 3.24 **Planning for a sub also includes collaborating with the class to discuss and define helpful behaviors ahead of time.**

enthusiastically volunteer. Don't hesitate for a second: thank them for being such eager volunteers and let them be that day's helpers. Now that they have taken the responsibility for helping the substitute, it is less likely that they—as hosts—will cause disruptions. Once you have your volunteers, discuss and make a class list of what being a sub helper entails. Students might suggest

- Introducing yourself at the beginning of the period.
- Helping the sub take attendance if necessary.
- Showing the substitute where to locate the lesson plans, seating charts, and needed supplies.
- Running errands if necessary.
- Reminding classmates it's the entire class' responsibility to host the sub with courtesy and patience; the sub will, of course, be unfamiliar with the way the class normally operates.

Write Up Your Plans

Whether you're turning in your just-in-case emergency plans or plans for a scheduled absence, keep them clear and useful by

1. **Making sure your seating charts are up-to-date.** Include the phonetic spelling of any student names that might be unfamiliar to the substitute.

2. **Typing up your sub plans and distributing copies.** Be specific in the details. Give a copy to the person in your building who is in charge of substitutes, give a copy to your immediate supervisor, and leave a copy in the classroom as well as a note on your desk stating where the plans are located. In case of a planned absence, also distribute a copy to your students before you're out.

Notice that the directions in Figure 3.25 portray the classes and students positively and that the sub is encouraged to read that positive description aloud to the class—most of the time, people live up to others' positive or negative aspirations for them (see Figure 3.26). Also, if something does go amiss, most substitutes are more than willing to take names and notes on any troublemakers without being asked.

Steineke—Sub Plans for November 4

(Periods 1, 2, 7)

Seating Chart: Located in right-hand desk drawer.

Please read aloud to class: First, second, and seventh hours are all pretty nice classes. A reminder to all students: remember to show our guest how great your friendliness and support skills are!

Have a good day!

STUDENT HELPERS (If you need assistance, these students are ready to help!)
1st: Motaz A., Freddy P.
2nd: Mike A., Charlie R.
7th: Jenna R., Emily K.

Academic English 10—1st, 2nd, 7th

1. **First 15 min.** Students should COMPLETE their Composition Book Piece (200-word minimum from topic determined by group on October 29). If the piece is completed, have students read library books and record this on the homework side of their reading logs.

2. Pass out student directions and have them read silently. Then continue with directions.

3. Students should move into their writing circles (see seating chart). Each student should take a turn reading the piece they wrote on November 1. After reading, each listening member should point out a specific word, phrase, or sentence that they liked as well as explaining in specific terms WHY they liked that part. The author should underline the words that were pointed out and take notes on the listener's reaction. When a group is finished discussing a piece, each member should have shared a specific "point-out" and the author should have three to four items underlined with accompanying notes.

4. Once a writing circle is finished listening to and responding to all the pieces, they should review their topic lists and negotiate a new writing topic for the group. The date (November 4) along with the topic should be written in the heading area of the next blank page located in the WRITING/READING section of the composition book. After determining the topic, members should discuss what they will be writing about and how they will narrow the topic down. Please observe and jot down names of students who do not have a new piece written to share.

5. If time remains, groups should adjourn, returning tables and chairs to their original position. Students may silently use the remaining time to read their SSR books or begin working on writing their new piece in their composition books. Remind everyone that the reading logs are due on November 5.

Figure 3.25 **When writing sub plans, be specific and positive. While it's sometimes common practice to warn subs about potential troublemakers, instead list the names of students who have volunteered to help.**

Figure 3.26 **If your students are committed to the plan, they might even carry through on their own!**

Dealing with a Bad Substitute Report

Even with the best of planning, you may get a report back from a substitute teacher that is less than glowing. And when you return, the students may blame their bad behavior on the sub's bad attitude and antagonistic classroom demeanor, accurate or not (see Figure 3.27). In the first moments of your return, it will be difficult to ascertain what actually happened, and an extended all-class rehash of the day's events may not be productive. Here's a quick example of what to try:

> *I wasn't there, but it certainly sounds as though things didn't go as planned. Let's try to figure out how we can deal with what happened while I was away and how we can ensure that the next time goes better. I'm going to give you a couple of silent minutes to reflect and write on the prompts that I've projected [see Figure 3.28]. Work on your own, recording your thoughts and ideas in writing.*

Figure 3.27 **Reflecting on a sub report can help you plan for your next absence. If you find that negative events were clearly instigated by the substitute, it's important to talk with an administrator.**

Part 1

- From your perspective, what went well while I was away?
- What didn't?

Part 2

- The next time there is a sub, what can you personally do to help make the day go well?

Part 3

- What can I do before the next sub day to help make the day go well?

Figure 3.28 **When a class gets a less than glowing review from a substitute, treat it as a time for learning and reflection rather than punishment.**

After students have written, collect all the sheets (make sure students have put their names on them) and thank your students for seriously thinking about how to solve this problem. Read through the responses for your own insights, but also save them to return to the students a little later, when the incident has had some time to fade into distant memory.

When you pass the reflections back, focus the talk on how to work more positively and collaboratively the next time the class encounters a substitute. And then move on to creating or modifying the "Working Successfully with a Substitute Teacher" T-chart. Also, if you seriously think that some of the class' problems were instigated by the substitute's poor behavior choices, it's important that you talk with an administrator before asking the substitute coordinator not to assign that person to your classroom again. However, never share personnel interventions with your students. The plan you just made is meant to prepare them for successfully and positively dealing with any challenging substitute who might be assigned to them in your absence.

How's It Going?

As you kid-watch and watch yourself, too, what are you seeing?

- ☐ I'm aiming for as many impromptu quick student conversations as I can get in as I greet kids at the door before class or as I visit with students at the end of class as they pack up.

- ☐ I've returned to those student interest surveys and made note of our specific commonalities.

- ☐ I think about what students need (from their perspective) as I plan lessons and assess their work.

- ☐ I'm noticing that students are becoming more comfortable interviewing and working with those they do not know well.

- ☐ I'm recognizing students' special talents.

- ☐ Students have embraced the norm of home court.

- ☐ Students are starting to enjoy using the skill of friendliness and support, maybe even overusing it (which is a good thing).

- ☐ Students are actively looking at and referring to the class norms posters as they work together.

Hey, look at you go! If you checked one box, you are on your way! Keep watching. Keep observing. Take every success, no matter how small, as a celebratory moment. And when a setback occurs, that's the signal to review the norms together with your students, revising and problem-solving as needed.

4

The Rest of the Year

SUPPORTING A STABLE AND PRODUCTIVE CLASSROOM ENVIRONMENT

Fifth-grade teacher Melissa Hoeft had a student, Jenny, who was always receptive and respectful to her, yet remained distant, sometimes perched on the edge of disruption. She entered fifth grade with a warning from previous teachers: "Many times she's not the drama instigator, but she manages to find herself a part of it." While Jenny never argued, she maintained a guarded presence with Melissa. Melissa tells the story of what happened on the day when the wall Jenny had built around herself cracked:

One day Jenny came in, flopped onto her desk, and just started sobbing. I called her out in the hall and asked her to tell me what was going on. I knew it had to be something beyond the typical fifth-grade drama due to how upset she looked. Jenny confided in me that her mom had to be rushed to the hospital the night before and she hadn't been able to speak with her mom since. Having lost my mom a few years earlier, I felt like I knew the pain and fear that this girl was feeling. I asked her one question that I feel was the turning point in our relationship. "What do you need from me?" She looked at me, paused for what felt like a full minute, and simply said, "I'm so tired, Mrs. Hoeft." I brought her back into my room, gave her a little pillow and an extra sweatshirt, and told her she could lie down behind my desk. She did and fell asleep. She slept for two hours curled up behind my desk. She

missed math, science, and some reading instruction, yet I could not have cared less.
I know some teachers would have given her a hug and then demand that she trudge
through the day. But, honestly, how would that response have helped Jenny? All it
would have done is show her that her trauma means nothing compared to adding
and subtracting decimals. Jenny's mom ended up being just fine after a day in the
hospital. From that day forward, Jenny made a point of giving me a hug. Every.
Single. Day. She was glued to my side and would often confide in me. Building
that level of trust means more to me (and her) because without it, academics are
a lost cause.

Supporting a Stable Environment All Year Long

In every classroom, students need to have trustworthy relationships with fellow students and with their teacher. Melissa's story demonstrates that students are observant, even if they are hesitant to share or if they seem wary. Through her daily positive, trustworthy teacher behavior, Melissa demonstrated that she could be trusted to hear a student's problem and take it seriously. If she had not already shown that she was trustworthy and reliable, it's unlikely that Jenny would have confided in her. Then Melissa listened and, rather than giving advice or a directive, asked a question that conveyed unconditional support: "What do you need from me?" Jenny's trust in Melissa let her reply honestly. And when she curled up behind Melissa's desk (the only available location for a nap), she trusted that she could take Melissa up on her offer without the fear that classmates might make fun of her later—she knew that Melissa and the class could be trusted with that, too.

While older students might choose a different solution than napping behind a teacher's desk, a teacher's listening and offering unconditional support without judgment is just as important to a twelfth grader as it is to a fifth grader. It is the support that students feel from those around them that enables everyone to succeed socially and academically. And it is this same support that can help students survive and arise from possibly soul-crushing events.

A strong, trusting community, one in which the students and the teacher work together to maintain a classroom that is welcoming and safe, has other benefits, as well. As students learn more about one another and become more interested in one another, they feel both the safety and the responsibility of being part of a community: Their small-group and whole-class discussions become stronger and more autonomous. They learn to recognize how their own behavior contributes to or detracts from the community and from their own academic success. They are more likely to give you and one another the benefit of the doubt when there is a problem. Having a strong classroom community doesn't mean that there is never a disruption in class, but it does mean that disruptions are more likely to be resolved quickly with understanding and trust than to be resolved bitterly with coercion and compliance.

In the previous chapters, we've worked on establishing this friendly, supportive community. Yet even the best relationships can fade or weaken if we don't give them attention—this is as true in our classrooms as it is in our lives beyond the classroom. Now that the first few weeks have passed and you are working on the semester's academic content, it's easy to forget that without the right environment students will learn and remember very little. It's up to us to keep our community relationships a priority throughout the entire year. We can do this in three ways. First, we can continue to provide opportunities for students to expand their acquaintanceships with us and with one another. Second, we can help acquaintanceships blossom into warm working friendships by giving student the tools and opportunities they need to actively value one another and celebrate one another's successes. Third, we can give them opportunities to recognize their own personal accomplishments and to set new, attainable goals.

The moves in this chapter work toward all three of these goals. You will reap fuller rewards if you implement at least one lesson from each of the three sections in this chapter and if you keep this work going throughout the entire year, actively using moves from this book on at least a weekly basis. By expanding acquaintanceship, you and your students will build stronger relationships with one another. One of the primary reasons students disrupt class or derail class is because they feel no investment in the teacher or their classmates. While occasional problems or disruptions will always occur due to the nature of adolescents and the nature of humans in general, they will be greatly diminished when interpersonal relationships are strong. Even though we teachers are always tempted to cut corners timewise in order to cover more content, devoting the necessary time to building relationships and celebrating the contributions of others is critical.

GOAL	MOVES
Expand Acquaintanceship	• Open Up Dialogues Using Letter Writing (page 108) • Make Time to Confer with Students About What Matters to Them (page 112) • Help Students Get to Know One Another's Interests and Areas of Expertise (page 117) • Ensure That Everyone Knows One Another's Name (page 121) • Make New Groupings and Change Seating on a Regular Basis (page 123)
Value and Appreciate Classmates	• Recognize Student and Family Expertise (page 128) • Name What Group Members Have in Common (page 132) • Appreciate Others' Contributions (page 136) • Celebrate Learning Together (page 141)
Strengthen Student Accountability	• Make Group-Work Work (page 147) • Heighten Students' Understanding of Their Own Collaboration Skills (page 151) • Guide Students in Academic Self-Evaluation and Goal Setting (page 154)

Goal: Expand Acquaintanceship

Lessons to support this goal:

- Open Up Dialogues Using Letter Writing (page 108)

- Make Time to Confer with Students About What Matters to Them (page 112)

- Help Students Get to Know One Another's Interests and Areas of Expertise (page 117)

- Ensure That Everyone Knows One Another's Name (page 121)

- Make New Groupings and Change Seating on a Regular Basis (page 123)

TRADITIONAL APPROACH	COLLABORATIVE APPROACH
• Teacher communication is limited to the comments written on papers and ad hoc interactions. • The seating chart may remain static for a course. Students may work together, but acquaintanceship depends on the skills they bring to the group.	• Students have regular opportunities to communicate with the teacher via writing and conferring. • The teacher deliberately structures opportunities for students to get to know and work with all their classmates.
⬇ LEADS TO ⬇	⬇ LEADS TO ⬇
∅ Students and the teacher may remain detached from one another. ∅ The quality of student collaboration is inconsistent. A class that enters already socially skilled is successful, while students without those skills flounder as the teacher becomes disenchanted with group work.	✔ Students recognize that the teacher is interested in them as individuals. ✔ Through acquaintanceship and collaborative work, a cohesive classroom community emerges.

Figure 4.1

MOVE>Open Up Dialogues Using Letter Writing

Immediate Result: Letters offer a way for students to share what's important to them in a more personal way than a quick conference or greeting chat.

Long-Term Result: Regular letter writing and responding is another way for you to build stronger rapport and deeper rapport with your students as you share with each other in written one-on-one conversations.

Begin by introducing the assignment. For example:

Today, I'd like you to write a letter to me. I know I've had quick chats with all of you, but a letter gives you the chance to share what's important to you in more detail, and that helps me know you better so that I can teach better. But the biggest reason I'm eager for you to write these letters is that I enjoy responding to your thoughts and writing back to you! While I can't promise to write each of you an individual letter because there's only one of me, I can promise that I will write you notes back on your letter, so when you write, be sure to leave some room in the margins for me. But I've also got to warn you that you won't be receiving those responses tomorrow. In the old days, when people mailed letters, they learned to be patient because it might take the receiver a few weeks to respond. So I'm asking for your patience as well so that I can really savor your writing and be thoughtful as I write back to you.

I may want to share some of the things I learn about you with the class—maybe that you're from a different city or that you love soccer. If there's anything that you put in your letter that you do not want shared with the class, just mention that in the letter: circle the parts that are just for me and write "do not share!" in the margin.

I'm posting some questions you might use to get started. Instead of giving short answers to all the questions, just pick two or three that you can really answer in detail. Also, please write legibly and do your best with spelling, grammar, and punctuation. I won't be grading you on those things, but the clearer your writing is, the easier it is for me to understand what you are trying to tell me.

How long does this letter have to be? Long enough for you to thoroughly tell me about yourself. Once you have finished writing, read your letter over to be sure that it says what you wanted to say.

Below are example prompts that you might let the students choose from, but feel free to make up your own questions instead. As with the interest inventory questions (see Figure 2.14, page 50), consider questions that *everyone* can answer and that are likely to lead to interesting responses. You might even want to leave the topics of the letters entirely up to the students.

A LETTER ABOUT ME

1. What's going on with you? What have you been devoting your time to lately? Have you gone anyplace special? Have you had any memorable moments?

2. How's the school year going so far? What have been the high points? Low points? Changes? What are your goals and plans?

3. What are you an expert in outside of school? What are your favorite hobbies, sports, music, and son on? Tell me about your interests, family, pets, future plans.

4. Have you always lived here? If so, what do you like about this area? If not, where have you lived before? What do you notice that's the same or different in this new neighborhood compared to the other places you lived?

5. Tell me about a time you wanted to learn how to do something and really enjoyed the process. It doesn't have to be school related. What were you learning? Why were you interested in this? Who was teaching you? How did it go?

6. What questions do you have for me? Your questions will give me some ideas for writing back to you!

After students have finished their letters, do not try to read all of them at once (unless you have a single, self-contained classroom). Since class loads for middle school and high school teachers often reach 150—or more—students, it's best to stagger this assignment, having only one class write letters at a time. Completely read, savor, and respond before the next batch of letters from a different class rolls in. As you read, you might underline some items you find interesting and unique. Rather than writing full letters back to each student—something that would likely keep you from replying in a timely manner—you can respond in marginal notes and perhaps a quick note at the end of the student's letter (see Figure 4.2). Then, as with the interest surveys, pick out

Wow— I hope your family was okay! That's scary!

My name is Deandre. I have not lived here for my whole. I actually lived in Harvey. I moved because while I was in Harvey on Christmas day we were robbed. So over the years we kept moving and moving to different places, and to be honest Oak Forest is far way more better than Harvey.

When school is over, I do football and that takes three hours and it sucks because when I get home it's 7:00 and to be honest I sometimes don't really get any free time because I have to shower, do my homework, then sleep. *You've got to be pretty devoted for football, but it sounds like you are doing a good job managing your time!*

My family is pretty crazy and funny and I really love them to death. I had a German Shepherd named Brucey growing up, but I don't really remember what happened to him. My grandma has a Bichon Frise named Nizzle and had him for six years now but he is now blind. Some years after that my cousins got a Doberman Pinscher named Nino and we were like best friends but he sadly died that same year they got him and I was really sad at that time. My friends are really good people and we got each other's back.

My school year is going good now though I do wish we still had summer vacation. What's gonna be different is school work. Last year we had work after work and most of the work didn't really mean anything to us because it was useless. When I was a freshman I was always good student, definitely to my teachers. The classes that I struggled the most were math and biology. For this year, I'm looking forward for everything because it will be nothing like freshmen year. I know for a fact that it's gonna be more fun. *What makes being a sophomore so much better than being a freshman?*

Something that happened over the summer was when my oldest brother got a dog. He got an Australian Shepherd and he named him Logan and there's a reason for that. Logan is a cool, wild, funny and trained dog and I love him.

Deandre,
Now I'm curious. What is the "reason" behind Logan's name? I once had a Scottie named Geraldine. This was in junior high when I had a crush on this guy named Jerry. We "went out" for about three weeks, but the dog lived to twelve!
Mrs G

Sincerely,

Deandre

Figure 4.2 **This teacher responds to Deandre's letter as if she were listening to him talk in real time, expressing interest, asking a question, or making connections as they arise. If your students have 1:1 computer access, they can type and post their letters for your digital responses.**

a few shareable items from a few letters each day to use in your greetings of specific students, striking up some brief conversations. This demonstrates to students that you do read and remember what they have to say. Don't bring up anything marked "private" in front of other students. And before you return the letters, create a list of names along with these items so that you can use the information in a later personalized "Find Someone Who" class-building activity (see Help Students Get to Know One Another's Interests and Areas of Expertise, page 117).

Finally, if you can swing it, make this letter writing a regular assignment, aiming for one letter from each student each quarter. You'll find the effort you take reading and responding to your students this way is far more enjoyable and productive than the time you take reading and grading other types of assignments. To make the time for the letters, you've got to think about what not to grade or, better yet, how students can be more involved in their own self-assessment and goal setting, addressed on pages 154–159.

MOVE>Make Time to Confer with Students About What Matters to Them

> **Immediate Result:** You have a quick, one-on-one conversation with a student in which they have your undivided attention: a clear demonstration that you are interested in each student as an individual.
>
> **Long-Term Result:** Making a habit of conferencing offers opportunities for expanding teacher–student acquaintanceship as well as opportunities for academic reflection. Additionally, if behavior issues arise, it will be easier to work with students with whom you've already conferenced.

No matter what subject you teach, at some time in your career you've likely tried one-to-one conferencing with students. A strong conference can be a powerful teaching move in any content area: you can use it to give kids exactly the support they need, to assess their progress, or to give feedback. But conferences don't always have to be about academic work: you can give students the option to talk about whatever they'd like to bring up with you, too—perhaps a question about something that happened in class, a conversation about why you've been seeing their head on their desk so often recently, or a play-by-play of the game their team won last night. When you make time to talk with students about what they want to talk about, you are showing them that they are a priority, and you're strengthening your connection with them.

You'll notice that in the previous paragraph I wrote that you've "likely tried" to confer. Here's the unfortunate follow-up to that statement: if you're like most teachers I know, you probably don't confer regularly—it is just too overwhelming to do consistently. No argument, there are quite a few obstacles to student conferencing: short periods, large class sizes, the challenge of trying to focus on a conference while simultaneously trying to unobtrusively extinguish off-task behavior with a pointed glance. I too gave up on conferencing until I came across an insight from teacher, researcher, and author Katie Wood Ray, which I'm paraphrasing: Even if you only get to each student two times over the entire school year, that would be two more conferences than I had with any of my own teachers from first grade through twelfth (Ray and Laminack 2001, 158).

So how can we make quick teacher–student conferencing work? Think of it as a check-in. What's one question you can ask that will get your students talking about themselves or your content in a personal and reflective way? You might ask:

- How's it going?
- What's something important that's going on in your life?
- What should I be watching/listening to/reading?
- Tell me about . . .
- What's something you like doing in this class?
- What's something you're better at now than you were at the start of the year?
- What did we talk about last time?

You really don't need a lot of questions. The point is for you to get a student talking and for you to listen and get to know that student better. Let the student drive the conversation. If they want to talk about something content related, that's fine. If they want to tell you about their new dog, that's fine, too. Do not fall into the pit of teacher-splaining. This is an opportunity for students to have their teacher's attention all to themselves for a few minutes. Your talking is limited to asking follow-up questions and possibly interjecting a momentary personal connection. If you feel like you talked too much, then you probably did. You want to leave knowing the student better rather than having offered a content-related minilesson or an academic goal they should shoot for.

The next issue is time: How long should a conference be, and how can we fit this conferencing into an already crowded period? Because we teachers like to talk, conferences often take longer than they need to. Keep the focus squarely on student sharing and aim for individual conferences running no longer than 3 minutes. If you can develop a 10-minute routine curricular individual activity that continues from day to day, you should be able to conference with three to five students during those 10 minutes.

Some of the conferencing advice I've run across recommends elaborate (and time-consuming) note-taking. A quicker way—and one that will help you offer as many conference opportunities to students as you can—is to have the students keep their own notes. When you have finished with the conference, hand the student a sticky note with the instruction "I want you to write down today's date and as much as you can remember about what we talked about, and then put the sticky on your official conference record" (which is just a plain sheet of paper with the heading "Official Conference Record")." If you want to get fancy, you can use a date stamp to put the date on a few sticky notes before you start conferring.

The only record you need to keep is a student roster on which you check off names as you conference. When every name is checked off, it's time to start a new roster and begin the next conference round. Of course, in subsequent conferences you can then begin by asking the student to refresh your memory and tell you what was covered in the previous conference. It's best to have students keep their conference record near the top of their folder or notebook so that the notes can be easily accessed. And of course, if your class has 1:1 devices, students can keep their conference record electronically.

The biggest stumbling block to conferencing is our concern that the rest of the class will quickly move off task. Solving this problem means turning back to the class for help. You might say something like

> *This year I'd really like to start conferencing with everyone in the class one-to-one. The conferences will be short, only about 2–3 minutes, and I'll usually be asking you what you want to talk about. My goal is to do quick check-ins with each of you in order to get to know you a little better, to have a better idea of how things are going for you in class, and to learn from you so that I can become a better teacher. I'm hoping to talk with three or four students most days, but to do that I need about 10 minutes of time when I can focus on those students without being distracted. What's something interesting, engaging, and related to this class that everyone else could work on silently and independently for 10 minutes so that I can have time to talk to you and your classmates? My initial ideas are independent choice reading or working on your ongoing projects. What are some ideas of yours we can add?*

Once you've worked with students to build a list, you'll need to determine which, if any, activities are required rather than optional. Melissa Hoeft, a fifth-grade teacher, gives students a sheet every couple of weeks delineating these work categories (see Figure 4.3). Yet even for the "Must Do" work, Melissa's students decide what they will

Name _____

MATH WORKSHOP CHECKLIST

Start: _____

Due: _____

Must Do—Turn In	Go Beyond
PearsonRealize.com ☐ 10–3 Visual Learning Bridge ☐ 10–3 Practice Buddy	☐ Solve Me Mobiles ☐ Division Slides ☐ Exploding Dots ☐ Khan Academy MAPPERS ☐ Catch Up on Math Topic Slides ☐ Watch other people's playlists on classroom ☐ Pick a game from the game crates and play with a friend

Must Do—Turn In

PearsonRealize.com
☐ 10–3 Visual Learning Bridge
☐ 10–3 Practice Buddy

Math Topic Slides
☐ Cube vs. Cubic Unit—differences and similarities
☐ Define with examples—Rectangular Prism
☐ Define volume and how we solve volume

Buddy Game
☐ Volume Puzzles

Create a YouTube Playlist
☐ Topic: Finding volume of rectangular prisms
☐ At least 2 videos about finding volume and 2 videos about rectangular prisms
☐ Comment on YOUR post: What is something you find difficult with finding volume, and how did one of the videos SPECIFICALLY help you work through that problem?

Volume Sheet
☐ In hanging chart
☐ Turn in when done

Khan Academy Mappers
10 minutes—3 times per week

Week 1	**Week 2**
☐ Day 1	☐ Day 1
☐ Day 2	☐ Day 2
☐ Day 3	☐ Day 3

Go Beyond

☐ Solve Me Mobiles

☐ Division Slides

☐ Exploding Dots

☐ Khan Academy MAPPERS

☐ Catch Up on Math Topic Slides

☐ Watch other people's playlists on classroom

☐ Pick a game from the game crates and play with a friend

Check the days you met with a teachers:

Week 1	**Week 2**
☐ Monday	☐ Monday
☐ Tuesday	☐ Tuesday
☐ Wednesday	☐ Wednesday
☐ Thursday	☐ Thursday
☐ Friday	☐ Friday

Figure 4.3 **While Melissa Hoeft develops the list of "Must Dos" based on curricular requirements, she works with students to develop the "Go Beyond" list located in the right-hand column.**

CONFERENCING TIME	
Looks Like	**Sounds Like**
• Class materials out and ready for use • Working individually • Focusing on work • Ignoring other students' conferences	• Quiet • Asking questions before or after conference time, not interrupting someone else's conference • Using soft voice during a conference

Figure 4.4 **You can post or project a T-chart like this one to remind students of expectations during conferring time.**

work on day to day during conference time, but they also know when those certain "Must Do" assignments are due. Offering students the choice to create their own work schedules enables them to change up their routines, but it also increases ownership of conference time quiet work while decreasing distracting behaviors. During teacher–student conferencing, students are free to complete the work in whatever order they desire. On some days they may choose to work on "Must Dos" while on other days they may choose work from the "Go Beyond" list. But every student clearly understands that they are responsible for completing and turning in the "Must Dos" by the designated due date. Melissa's checklists not only give her time to confer, but they also offer her students options for how they will spend their time in class.

Once you've negotiated the individual work, the next step is to work with students to develop a T-chart that defines what conferencing time should look like and sound like in your classroom (see Figure 4.4). The final management tip for conferencing is to avoid the inclination to stay at your desk and have students come to you. Instead, get a light chair or stool that you can easily move around the room. Sitting at eye level with students instead of standing above them facilitates conversation. Additionally, moving into the students' space discourages students from falling off task and eliminates the need for students to get out of their seats, which can distract others (Figure 4.5).

Figure 4.5 **Lindsey Jones pulls up a chair to this eighth grader's table as she asks him what he wants to talk about. This student chose a journal entry that was particularly important to him.**

MOVE>Help Students Get to Know One Another's Interests and Areas of Expertise

Immediate Result: Students enjoy a fun activity with their classmates and recognize you have read their "get to know me" letters carefully.

Long-Term Result: Students gradually get to know all their classmates in brief, low-risk interactions. Students learn about their classmates' unique talents, experiences, and interests in a way that builds mutual admiration and interest in one another. Students will feel as though their classmates are people they know, not strangers—this makes future whole-class participation, group work, discussions, and student presentations easier for all involved.

One of the best ways I've seen to help a group of people get to know one another quickly is to try an activity called "Find Someone Who." To set up this activity, start by creating a three-column chart with these headings: "Unique Facts," "My Classmate's Name," and "Interview Details." Then start reviewing the interesting details you underlined in the letters students wrote to you. Pick a few distinctive items for each student, ones that no other student shares and that were not marked as "private." Then type these items. Don't forget to include a line with some unique details about you! Figure 4.6 shows part of what a finished document might look like. Once the form is completed, you can either duplicate copies for everyone or disseminate it electronically so that students can use their devices to make their notes (see Figure 4.7). Then ask a student volunteer to model the following procedure with you:

1. Step away from your desk.

2. Silently raise your hand to find a new partner.

3. Pair up and introduce yourselves. Decide who will be interviewed first.

Period 5 Find Someone Who

Find Someone Who	My classmate's name is . . .	Their answer to my question (use a complete sentence here)
Moved here from Indiana just a year ago and is thinking about trying out for the golf team.		
Grew up in Orlando, Florida, and would someday like to be a cosmetologist.		
Is in marching band and was very disappointed this summer when their favorite band didn't show up at a music festival.		
Is a *serious* baseball player and admires their father's hard work and determination.		
Recently went to Florida for a wedding and also went to Disney.		
Grew up in Poland and plays football.		
Loves to draw and loves their mom.		
Has six brothers and one sister and *really* wants a dog.		
Got a new puppy over the summer and scored the winning point in a huge basketball tourney.		
Helps their younger siblings with homework after school and has fallen on their face—literally!		
Used to attend Stagg High School and has a pit bull named Rocky.		
Plays football, loves their dog, and used to live in San Diego, California.		
Loves dancing and recently went downtown for their birthday.		
Has four German shepherds and likes to hang out at McCarthy Park.		

My classmate's name is . . .	Their answer to my question (use a complete sentence here)
Traveled to the East Coast last summer and is taking two AP classes this year.	
Is a country music–obsessed cheerleader who wants to be a pediatric nurse someday.	
Plays softball and has a new baby sister!	
Likes skateboarding, comic books, and was bit by a dog on their face.	
Regularly travels to Florida and Las Vegas to visit family and has a brother named Cosmo.	
Has cheated death twice and has pet rats.	
Is good with computers and *really* wants to sit near Jennet and Tasha.	
Spends summers in Ireland, plays water polo, and once back flopped off of a rope swing.	
Is interested in philosophy and scared of horses.	
Can shake their eyes and fixes bikes for cash.	
Plays tennis, will join Project Diversity, and went to Wisconsin Dells over the summer.	
Hopes to be a firefighter someday and is on the VJA bowling team.	
Used to live in California and enjoys boxing and basketball.	
Plays Wiffle ball in the backyard with their grandpa and went to the Louisville Slugger bat factory over the summer.	

Figure 4.6 This is one example of a personalized Find Someone Who search. All the items listed are unique, taken from the letters of introduction written earlier. Students are usually delighted to find their own details as well as those of their classmates.

4. The interviewee points out their unique facts and the interviewing partner writes down the fact owner's first and last name. It's fine to ask fact owners to spell out their names so that the recording is accurate, but it is *not okay* for fact owners to grab the paper or device and write their own name. The point of the interviewer writing the name is that they are more likely to remember their classmate's name later.

5. After recording the name, the interviewer asks some questions to learn more about one or more of the facts listed. Then the interviewer records those details in the third column.

Figure 4.7 **Sophomore students in Colleen Ghelfi's classroom record their partners' names and interview information on an online form.**

6. Once an interview is completed, the roles switch.

7. After both interviews, partners thank each other for the conversation and find new partners by raising their hands and looking around to find someone else who has their hand up.

Since students will have already had experience interviewing partners using previous activities described in Chapters 2 and 3, you probably will need to only quickly review how to ask open-ended questions that result in interesting answers. Also, remind students that these are quick interviews and that they should talk only with one partner at a time. Even though you are on the sheet, you might consider limiting your actual "Find Someone Who" participation to the days when there are an odd number of students. That way, there is no need for trios.

Trying to complete the sheet in a single day can be overwhelming. It's best to limit the search to about five people per day—perhaps about 10 minutes of class time. As you observe and coach, you may notice an item that is consistently blank. In that case, it's okay to intervene, directing students to those who hold the secrets related to those blank items.

MOVE>Ensure That Everyone Knows One Another's Name

> **Immediate Result:** By writing a list of classmates, students tangibly begin to observe who they know by name and who they don't.
>
> **Long-Term Result:** Revisiting the list and adding names gives students a sense of accomplishment as well as increasing their sense of belonging and community.

Many times, we assume that students know one another's names when, in actuality, they don't—even if they've been in the same school for years. When students are changing classes every hour or so, the classmates are less likely to know one another's names. And the bigger the school, the bigger the odds of anonymity. When others know your name and address you by name, at the very least this is assurance that they see you as a person. More importantly, when people feel seen, they feel far more engaged with and committed to their classmates and the work at hand.

Start this activity by explaining the importance of knowing everyone by name. You might point out that knowing people by name makes it easier to work together, makes it less scary to work in a new group, and creates a greater sense of community. Then launch students into the activity:

> *So, let's see how we're doing with knowing each other's names. Grab a piece of paper and number one through (the number of people in the class plus the teacher). Now, totally on your own, start writing down the first and last names of your classmates and my name, as well. It's okay to look around at faces if you need a memory trigger, but it's not okay to ask for anyone's help or distract others as they try to think. See how many people you know by name.*

As students write, monitor their progress in order to get a grasp of where they are with knowing their classmates by name (see Figure 4.8). Don't be tempted to ask for a show of hands in regard to how many names students were able to list or to ask students to identify whose names they don't know. The goal of this exercise is not to determine which students know the most names but to help all the students consider how well they know their classmates. To help students see this as a way for them to check their own knowledge of their peers, not as a competition, explain:

> *As I walked around the room just now while you were working, I noticed that no one was able to list everyone correctly. So here's your challenge: every time you come into class, make it a goal to learn a new name by getting to know a new person. If you're a little shy, don't worry. I'm making it my goal to give you the chance to work with everyone else in this room by the time this course is over.*

Figure 4.8 Remembering names takes some concentration.

Revisit the list every time you change groups, encouraging students to revise the spelling of those they previously listed as well as add new names to their list. Another time to revisit the list is after a few rounds of "Find Someone Who" (see Help Students Get to Know One Another's Interests and Areas of Expertise, page 117).

MOVE>Make New Groupings and Change Seating on a Regular Basis

Immediate Result: Students continue to expand their acquaintanceship of class-mates on a regular basis.

Long-Term Result: As students work with others and become more socially skilled, meeting new people becomes more comfortable. Students can focus on the work at hand rather than their unease about working with strangers. Ideally, students develop new friendships as well.

Every three to four weeks, or when a unit of study has concluded, it's time to change seats and groupings. I recommend continuing to assign groups rather than let-ting kids pick their own. Unfortunately, when left to their own devices, people will choose to work with those they know while others end up feeling ignored and left out. Besides the "anti-welcome" self-chosen groups create, they also eliminate the possibility of a discussion that includes diverse background knowledge, ideas, and viewpoints. Whether students or adults, people are attracted to their friends because they have a lot in common; they are more similar than they are different. While this comes in handy when trying to figure out what Netflix show to watch, similar viewpoints generally weaken an academic group. Additionally, as students transition into adulthood, they'll be working increasingly with groups they may not be able to choose: their bosses, college roommates, colleagues, committee members—the list could go on and on. Being able to work successfully with new people in new situ-ations is an important life skill. Assigned groups require students to learn how to break the ice and shape new working relationships positively.

At this point in the year, our goal is more than just "mixing kids up"—it's making sure that all students have the opportunity to work with all their class members throughout the course of the semester or year. Therefore, it's best to keep track of who has worked with whom while still aiming for a certain amount of surprise. A few days before students are ready to switch seats and partners for the very first time, I pass out copies of the class roster, duplicated with some extra space at the top for a little math (see Figure 4.9). After writing their first and last names, students list details of numeric importance:

- The number of people in their close family (when students ask whom they should include, just say, "If you consider someone part of your close family, count them. And yes, close family can include people with whom you are not blood related).

- An important date (birth date, parents' anniversary, graduation date, sister's wedding date, and so on).

- Their house or apartment number (if a student is unsure of their address number, have them use the school address number).

Figure 4.9 **Example of a completed roster**

Once the numbers are listed, students should separately add up the digits of the special date and the house number to get two totals. Adding the digits in the date—3/13/17—produces a sum of 15 (3 + 1 + 3 + 1 + 7). Adding the digits of the house number—5538—produces a sum of 21 (5 + 5 + 3 + 8). Last, students should add up the family member number plus the other two sums. In the example, the family member number is 5, so the total is 41 (5 + 15 + 21).

You'll notice that the process is intentionally complex: we want the numbers to be unguessable and unpredictable. Besides, the kids often get a kick out of the peculiarities of the elements in the equation.

When the math is completed, have students go through the class roster, crossing off their own name as well as the names of the one or two people they have worked consistently with during the last few weeks. Before the lists are turned in the first time, I also give them the option of crossing off one more name, explaining that if there is someone they'd prefer not to work with, they can cross that name off the list. If students feel this strongly about a classmate, it's doubtful that simply putting them in the same group, without any additional support, will be helpful. While I emphasize that I can't 100 percent guarantee that they'll never have to work with the individual, I do try to notice those extra cross-offs. Most kids do not cross off anyone, so take special note of the ones who do because those crossed-out names often indicate a serious and yet unresolved conflict that may be worth discussing with the student privately or with a guidance counselor.

After students complete their cross-offs, collect the lists and use the family numbers to order the rosters into a pile from the lowest to highest number. Grab four rosters from the pile in order to form a new group of four, double-checking that these students haven't worked together before. If you notice a repetition, just pull the next name and make an adjustment. Also, depending on your class composition, you might want to consider forming groups with greater diversity in gender, ethnicity, and so on. There is no deep and steadfast science to the group forming. Your goal as you put new groups together is to actively orchestrate the expansion of acquaintanceship. Finally, create your new seating charts, and assign students their new seats with their new groups.

A good time to change groups is when you enter a new unit of study—perhaps every three or four weeks. Each time new groups need to be formed, return the rosters so that students can cross off the names of those they've just worked with. Then, just as before, sort by number using a different sum. As you and the class work together for a longer period of time, you'll find that it becomes much more difficult to create groups of absolute "strangers." However, if each student is working with at least one or two new people, that is sufficient in growing the acquaintanceship.

As you look at groupings in each successive reorganization, consider: Has everyone in the class had opportunities to work with both the infinitely patient and friendly class members and the most challenging class members? Has everyone *consistently* had opportunities to work with students of a different gender and with students who have reached different levels of academic achievement?

Goal: Value and Appreciate Classmates

Lessons to support this goal:

TRADITIONAL APPROACH	COLLABORATIVE APPROACH
• Occasional sharing and awareness of family and student interests may happen, but is not planned. When students work in groups, the only focus is the academic task.	• Structure ways for students to share the interests and talents of themselves and their families.
• It is only the teacher's responsibility to recognize student contributions.	• Teach students to actively recognize the contributions of others and appreciate how these contributions influence their own success.
⬇ LEADS TO ⬇	⬇ LEADS TO ⬇
∅ When students work together in groups, their interaction will most often range from off-task to superficial because they have no investment in one another.	✔ As students know classmates better, their acquaintanceship expands, as does their ability to be empathetic and see situations from perspectives other than their own.
∅ Gaining a teacher's approval and praise becomes a competition. Some students will willingly compete and bask in the teacher's positive words, while others will drop out of the game early and quickly be labeled as lazy and unmotivated.	✔ When students feel appreciated and recognize one another for their contributions, they are much more likely to participate in class and be successful working in small groups.

Figure 4.10

MOVE>Recognize Student and Family Expertise

Immediate Result: Students consider the different funds of knowledge that people in their lives hold and enjoy a new method for connecting with classmates.

Long-Term Result: Students see themselves and their classmates as having something worthy to contribute. As topics arise throughout the school year, student and family experts can be consulted and recognized for their unique expertise, reconnecting the classroom to the social networks and resources of the community.

In the article "Funds of Knowledge for Teaching: Using a Qualitative Approach to Connect Homes and Classrooms," Luis Moll, professor of language, reading, and culture at the University of Arizona, and his colleagues observe that the knowledge, intelligence, and experience of minoritized children and their families were often underestimated (Moll et al. 1992). As Moll and his colleagues explain:

> *Our analysis of funds of knowledge represents a positive (and, we argue, realistic) view of households as containing ample cultural and cognitive resources with great potential utility for classroom instruction. This view of households, we should mention, contrasts sharply with prevailing and accepted preceptions of working-class families as somehow disorganized socially and deficient intellectually; perceptions that are well accepted and rarely challenged in the field of education and elsewhere.*

Their research revealed that giving students' and families' abundant knowledge public light creates a richer classroom, an appreciation of culture and diversity, and an opportunity for teachers to use this knowledge for improved student learning.

In response, Moll and his colleagues developed a simple webbing activity that enables students to inventory and celebrate the far-reaching talents of their family members as well offering a way for other students and teachers to gain awareness and tap into this tremendous wealth of expertise.

To start, pass out blank pieces of paper and have students put their own name in the center. Next, have students add the names of those they consider family surrounding their name, spreading out the family names so that words can be added. Emphasize to students that family is whomever they consider family. Family can be related by blood—or not. If you consider your next-door neighbor family, then they are family. Period. Once students have listed their family members, they can start jotting down words and phrases that describe the knowledge and expertise each possesses. Emphasize that knowledge doesn't come from just school and books, and it isn't limited to academics. People learn much through living, working, and raising families. It is helpful if you quickly demonstrate your own thinking about family talents or prepare an example ahead of time to show the kids. Your examples will help your students see what you mean by "knowledge," so be sure to highlight a range of knowledge. Sure, you can mention your aunt who's a doctor or your friend who's a lawyer, but don't overlook your cousin who knows every backroad shortcut in your state, your uncle who can fix anything, or your neighbors who can speak three languages.

Encourage students to just think about what their family members know about and what they're good at. Sometimes it's helpful if they think about some different categories of how people learn—not only in school, but also from others they know, through life experiences, and through traditions or customs.

The bottom line is that there is no wrong answer. The more students think about the knowledge that surrounds them, the more they will add to their web (see Figures 4.11 and 4.12). Once students have explored these

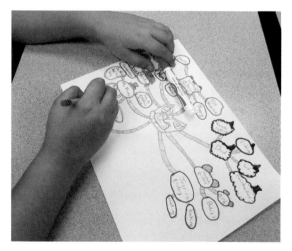

Figure 4.11 **Once students begin to think about those around them, creating a Funds of Knowledge map is an engaging experience.**

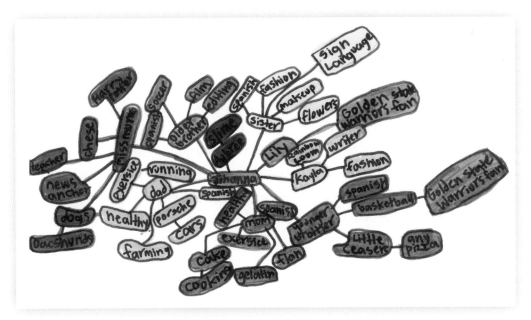

Figure 4.12 **As students work on their Funds of Knowledge maps, they include those they consider family, whether blood related or not.**

funds, the final step is for students to begin connecting knowledge between their own family members. Who else in their family plays an instrument? Bakes a great cake? Knows how to haggle at a flea market or garage sale? After completing the map in class, encourage students to take it home overnight and share it with their family members to see if they missed anything.

The following day, begin showing students how to use their Funds of Knowledge maps for a series of partner interviews following these steps:

1. Everyone stands up and finds a partner.
2. Partners trade maps and pick out something interesting. Then each partner in turn conducts a brief interview based on a family member's talents (see Figure 4.13).
3. When both partners have completed interviewing each other, they thank each other, return maps to their owners, and find a new partner.

While the interviewing commences, your job is to move from pair to pair, listening and learning. Also, if you find the interviewing timing too uneven (one pair is done in a minute, another is still talking 5 minutes later), it's fine to coordinate the timing of the pair changes by announcing how many minutes pairs have left to talk and then announcing when it's time to switch partners. And once the interviewing is concluded, post the maps publicly so that as topics in class arise, you and your students can refer to the expertise of those on the maps and, perhaps, invite those experts into the classroom to share what they know.

Figure 4.13 Once the Funds of Knowledge maps are completed, students can't wait to share, compare, and interview each other about each other's family talents.

MOVE>Name What Group Members Have in Common

Immediate Result: Newly formed groups begin their work together in a way that sets the stage for friendly collaboration.

Long-Term Result: Students recognize that diversity does not exclude commonality. When students see that they have much in common, positive relationships and friendships form more easily—and more quickly! Students and teacher see themselves as part of the same team, ready to face learning challenges together, ready to understand and support one another.

The flip side of celebrating the knowledge and experience diversity brings to the classroom is celebrating what students have in common. This idea works best when students have changed seats and have just begun working in a new group of four. Begin by duplicating the form in Figure 4.14 and Online Resource 4.1. Start modeling this activity by asking four student volunteers to step up to the front as you project the "What Do We Have in Common?" form. Have students stand in a line, and

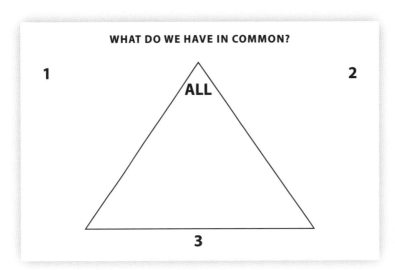

Figure 4.14 **This "What Do We Have in Common?" form makes it easy for groups to inventory their members' similarities.**

introduce the activity by saying, "Today we are going to take an inventory of our common interests, enthusiasms, and experiences within our new group. Watch how we do this." Then invite the first student in line to volunteer an interest of theirs. Immediately follow up by asking how many in the group share that interest, enthusiasm, or experience. Record the item on the form according to the number of people in the group who have the item in common (see Figure 4.15). Continue, cycling through the student volunteers in order a few times. See if students have any questions. Once groups are formed, tell students:

> I'm going to give you about 5 minutes to see how many things you can find that your group members have in common. Move quickly around the group. See how many times you can get to each member before I call time. When it's your turn, name an idea and write it down in the appropriate spot. Before moving on to the next member for another enthusiasm, interest, or experience, make sure everyone has written the previous item in the correct space on the sheet. Also, if you have a lot of ideas when it's your turn, pick the one that you think is most likely to end up in the "ALL" triangle. Any questions? Go!

If you and your students have already worked through the Funds of Knowledge move (see page 128), you might also suggest that they look at those webs for ideas. After about

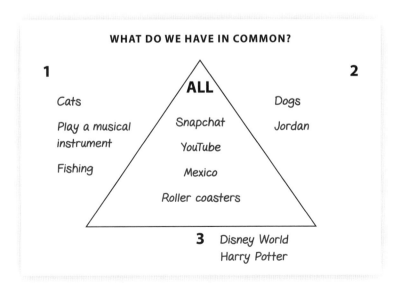

Figure 4.15 **Move through this activity quickly, generating as many ideas as possible in order to get a quick interest/experience inventory of the group.**

5 minutes—or sooner if it appears groups have found ample items they have in common—move on to the next step. Pass out markers and sheets of chart paper, giving these instructions:

> *Now that you have a pretty good idea of what you all have in common, how could you turn that knowledge into a group identity? Your job is to think of a name for your group that reflects something you have in common, then use illustrations to show your commonalities [see Figures 4.16 and 4.17]. As you work on the drawings, make sure everyone contributes. The point is not to have the best artist do all the work. The point is to have your poster represent the work and common interests of your entire group [see Figures 4.18 and 4.19].*

After students finish their posters, hang them on the wall and use them for impromptu gallery walks. For the first round, have half the groups stay by their posters while the other groups choose a poster for closer examination and interviewing opportunities. Encourage "gallery viewers" to ask questions, get details, and see what commonalities they share with members of other groups. After a few minutes, reverse the roles.

Figures 4.16 and 4.17 **The "Annoying Sisters Club" and the "Trampoline Squad" get to work, using their "What Do We Have in Common?" inventories as inspiration.**

Figures 4.18 and 4.19 **Museum-quality art is not the intention. Both of these posters include input and drawings from all members, thoughtful visual representations, and just enough mystery to invite curiosity and questions.**

Once students are familiar with the process of finding commonalities, this activity is a good way to jump-start new groups every time you change seats. Plus, when the old posters come down, new ones go up, so your gallery displays rotate rather than becoming wallpaper. The idea of finding commonalities can also be applied to content areas as groups examine what they know about or have in common regarding a topic or event (see Figure 4.20).

Figure 4.20 **These fifth-grade students charted their interests as readers as they prepared to make a book choice that would interest all the members of their book club.**

MOVE>Appreciate Others' Contributions

Immediate Result: Taking the time to explicitly acknowledge positive contributions of other classmates helps everyone feel appreciated by and important to their classmates.

Long-Term Result: Students who have consistently offered thanks and receive thanks will value the importance of this positive action and will be more likely to pay it forward to others in future work and social relationships—without prompting.

Young people who thank others and feel grateful have a more positive attitude toward school and higher grade point averages (Kapp 2013). However, kids often need to be taught thankfulness through modeling and practice. So how can we help students demonstrate gratitude to one another?

First, whenever students work together, give students a "thank you" prompt to use as the work concludes. Tell them to turn to their partners, address them by name, and then enthusiastically say the "thank you" prompt out loud. It's that simple!

Thank You Prompts

1. Thanks for working with me today.
2. Thanks for listening to my ideas.
3. Thanks for sharing your ideas.
4. Thanks for the great conversation on _____.
5. Thanks for your positive attitude.

You'll need only a few prompts: after you've used these up, you can have your students brainstorm new "thank you" prompts with their partners.

Next, a day or two before students change seats to meet new partners and form new groups, have students write thank-you notes to each of their current members. You might start the discussion by asking students if they have ever received a thank-you note (probably very few have). Then ask how many students have ever written a thank-you note (probably a few more, who were most likely nagged by an adult to do so). Finally ask, "Why is it so difficult to write thank-you notes?" While procrastination will certainly be cited, someone is bound to say that they just don't know what to write, which opens up the discussion to what makes a good thank-you note. Some discussion of this will most likely bring up criteria that make a difference:

- *Timeliness:* The best time to thank someone is soon after the gift or favor is received.

- *Personalization:* Thanks should not sound like a form letter. It should be authentic and specific to the person's contribution and how that contribution made a difference in the receiver's life.

- *Length:* While thanking someone properly requires focus, it does not require great length. A simple statement of thanks may be direct and brief. A thank-you note need not be more than two or three sentences long.

Once students understand these principles, tell them it's time to write some notes themselves, one to each group member, highlighting something positive they contributed to the group and why it was personally important to them. Give students a few moments to consider what they are grateful to their group members for or what they have learned from them. Even group members who consistently disagree can likely find that they have learned something from one another—perhaps how they can disagree amicably. After students have worked out and revised their rough-draft notes on a few sheets of paper (this shouldn't take too long since each note is only two to three sentences long), pass out half sheets of colored paper along with some colored pencils or markers. Then let students pull their desks away from one another or create some private table space so that they can work individually to make the thank-you notes a surprise. Have students fold each half sheet into a card, "hamburger bun"-style, addressing the note on one of the outer sides and writing the note inside, below the fold (see Figures 4.21, 4.22, and 4.23). You might post the following reminders as students work.

As you get ready to write your letter, remember to

1. Leave the upper half of the card blank.
2. Write the date in the upper-right-hand corner.
3. Include an opening, a closing, and your signature.
4. Use the content tips (personalization/specificity and brevity) we talked about earlier.
5. Once you've finished writing your first thank-you note, continue writing one for each member of your group.

Figure 4.21, Figure 4.22, and Figure 4.23
Students' thank-you notes to their peers are powerful because they are specific and honest.

Dear Steven,

Bro this semester was really fun. I wish you weren't leaving because we work really well together, whenever we had to do something we are good at bouncing ideas back and forth. We both don't like talking in front of the class but you made me do it and I got you to do it. I hope that we have more classes together these next two years and thank you for all the help!

Merry Christmas,
Luke

DEAR RUMSEY,

RUMSEY YOU WERE ONE OF THE PEOPLE WHO KEPT OUR GROUP GOING WITH POSITIVE THOUGHTS. YOU WERE ALWAYS IN A GREAT MOOD AND KEPT US GOING. I JUST WANT TO SAY THANK YOU AND IT WAS A HONOR TO HAVE YOU IN MY GROUP.

LOVE,
Chris

Once students have finished writing their notes, have each student nest their two or three notes together, one inside the other. Then have students clip their notes together as a group and turn them in to you. This gives you the opportunity to skim through, enjoy the gratitude, and see what students value in one another. If you run across a gratitude-deficient note, have a conference with the student, help them consider ways in which they might be legitimately grateful to the addressee, and have them write a new note. Return the notes to the groups for distribution right before members disband for new seats and new partners.

In Sheila Furey Sullivan's senior acting class, students write thank-you notes throughout the semester. Then, on the last day before finals begin, Sheila delivers the notes by dropping them into lunch bags that the students have decorated and hung on the wall (see Figure 4.24). The kids retrieve their bags, and the notes offer them some souvenir memories and the opportunity to celebrate their time spent together.

Figure 4.24 **Sheila Furey Sullivan likes to use her students' thank-you notes as an end-of-year celebration.**

Figure 4.25

Later in the school year, once students have worked with and gotten to know most of their classmates, you can give kids an opportunity to show appreciation and gratitude in unison. Once a week, fifth-grade teacher Melissa Hoeft devotes a gratitude day to one classmate. In turn, every classmate steps up to the board and writes a positive contribution that student has made to their classmates (see Figure 4.25). Then, before the board is erased, she takes a picture of the student in front of their compliments (see Figure 4.26).

Figure 4.26 After students take turns noting how Anthony has made a difference to the rest of the class, Anthony takes his turn at the board, getting his photo taken with his compliments.

MOVE>Celebrate Learning Together

Immediate Result: Focusing on successes helps students feel comfortable and connected with one another.

Long-Term Result: Taking the class time to celebrate collaborative and learning successes creates a supportive environment in which students feel comfortable taking learning risks.

The most effective celebrations of learning aren't pizza parties or award ceremonies—they're continual acknowledgments of students' contributions and growth. Here are four ideas for how to keep celebrations part of every school day and include them at the end of the year.

1. Gestures of Affirmation

One of the factors that will help students achieve and succeed in your classroom is explicit proof that they are an appreciated part of the classroom community. Engagement and interest blossom when students are celebrated for their learning accomplishments, collaborative skillfulness, and academic risk taking. As teachers, we need to make our celebration just as important as our need to follow the curriculum. So how do we do this?

Sometimes, the best feedback comes from peers: we can teach the ritual of thanking group members and using positive, school-appropriate gestures, such as fist bumps or high fives (see Figures 4.27 and 4.28). You can brainstorm ideas for gestures together with your students (see Chapter 2, page 51). Every time students work together, they can end by thanking one another with words and a celebratory gesture. You will be surprised by how good you and your students feel at the end of class with just these quick, simple actions.

2. Photo Displays

Another way to celebrate classroom moments is with photos. Hang them on the inside of your door, making sure that everyone in the room is pictured in a couple of shots—and then watch the excitement as your students file in and see the photos (see Figure 4.29). These photos document the community as well as your interest in the students.

3. Public Performance Appreciation

One of the things we sometimes forget about when teaching is that our classroom offers us a built-in audience. So it behooves us to take advantage of this asset. Whenever possible, offer students the opportunity to celebrate learning in front of their peers. If your students have spent weeks writing research papers, don't just end that project by having them turn the papers in. Inform them from the beginning that they will be reading excerpts to the class. Not only will this increase individual investment in the project because the audience has expanded (really, who would devote hours and hours to a paper that is ultimately experienced by an audience of one?), but this public sharing helps students learn from one another. Note that this is not the same thing as delivering an oral report or a presentation—it's sharing just a bit of their work (the part they're proudest of) as a celebration. Of course, part of a performance celebration means discussing what it means to be a good audience member (see Figure 4.30). This skill can be defined with a T-chart, using the same steps outlined earlier in the move Teach Collaborative Skills Directly (Chapter 3, page 82).

Figure 4.27 **After some successful collaboration, these seventh-grade boys end their meeting with a celebratory high five.**

Figure 4.28 **These high school juniors are enjoying a group thumbs-up after a successful discussion of *The Great Gatsby*. Notice the genuine smiles. When students are taught to celebrate their collaboration, they begin to look forward to it!**

Figure 4.29 **High school teacher Sheila Furey Sullivan's interior classroom door features photos of her freshmen and senior students in action throughout the day in the various classes she teaches.**

GOOD AUDIENCE	
Looks Like	**Sounds Like**
• Interested	• Quiet attention
• Respectful	• Responding to speaker (when appropriate)
• Thoughtful/attentive	• Clapping (when appropriate)
• Sitting up straight	• Laughter (when appropriate)
• Smiling	• Saving conversation until AFTER performance
• Enjoying performance	
• Care about what's being said	
• Eye contact	
• Desk is clear	
• Hands and body still	

Figure 4.30 **As one might guess, body language comes into greater play than talking when being an audience member. When creating a T-chart, remember to keep the descriptors positive. Instead of saying, "No talking," it's better to say, "Save the conversation for later."**

Of course, after the performance, the celebration can extend beyond just applause. Those performing can choose what kind of cheer they would like to receive (see Figure 4.31). While class cheers are commonplace in elementary school, sadly they are often forgotten by middle and high school. But they shouldn't be! You would be surprised by how much seniors in high school enjoy requesting fireworks (clap your hands together for the explosion, raise your arms up, and then lower your arms, wiggling your fingers as the glowing embers fall back to earth) or roller coaster

Figure 4.31 **While students perform a scene in Sheila Furey Sullivan's senior acting and theatre class, the audience behaves respectfully. But after the applause dies down, it is the performers who turn to the audience and request their preferred celebratory cheer.**

(make a ratcheting sound as you lift your arms in front of you, pause at the top, and then make three consecutive up the hill and down the hill gestures with your arms while shouting "Woo! Woo! Woo!"). More traditional cheers include the wave or a rhythmic stadium stomp.

4. Certificates of Appreciation

When student groups are concluding their work together, consider playful certificates that highlight an important skill that each member brought to the table (see Figure 4.32). Here are some ideas to get you started.

WORLD'S BEST . . .

Orator

Future Lawyer

Follow-up Questioner

Figure 4.32 **Displaying the certificates they awarded each other upon the conclusion of their last meeting, this group of juniors developed such a strong bond in their literature circle that they wanted their group to stay together for the rest of the semester.**

Segue Spotter

Connection Finder

Friendliness and Support Champ

Book Club CEO

MVP (Most Valuable Player)

Historian

Encourager of Others

Once students are familiar with the "awards," you can work together to come up with additional categories and titles.

Goal: Strengthen Student Accountability

Lessons to support this goal:

- Make Group-Work Work (page 147)

- Heighten Students' Understanding of Their Own Collaboration Skills (page 151)

- Guide Students in Academic Self-Evaluation and Goal Setting (page 154)

TRADITIONAL APPROACH	COLLABORATIVE APPROACH
• Students are assigned to groups without consideration of the underlying social processes at play. • Students are expected to know how to work together in groups without receiving specific guidance or training.	• Student group work is carefully planned and structured by the teacher. • Interaction skills that enhance group functioning and academic achievement are explicitly taught, and students then monitor and improve their skill usage.
⬇ LEADS TO ⬇	⬇ LEADS TO ⬇
∅ The success of group work is inconsistent. Some groups that contain serendipitously skilled members flourish while other groups flounder, unable to complete the academic tasks. In turn, the teacher views group work as a strategy that can be used only with some classes and some students. ∅ Student collaboration skills remain static or decline; they are directly affected by the skills of other members. Students who are grade conscious and academically motivated are frustrated by less motivated members. These students develop an intense dislike for collaboration because they view it as inherently unfair.	✔ Students participate in group work activities that are "doable" given their current skill level and therefore find the experiences successful and rewarding. ✔ Students continually monitor and refine their interaction skills, allowing them to function in groups more effectively and complete more complex collaborative tasks. Also, as students understand and master the necessary components of successful collaboration, these skills will be carried on to future classes and careers.

Figure 4.33

MOVE>Make Group-Work Work

Immediate Result: Student collaboration will have a higher rate of productive on-task work as well as fewer hitchhikers.

Long-Term Result: Students will work in groups effectively. Students who have a negative perception of group work because of prior disappointing experiences will gradually revise their attitudes and value collaboration.

Group work is not always universally beloved. Comb through the comic strip *Dilbert* or search Google Images using the phrase "group work memes" and you will find that there appears to be a universal annoyance in regard to teamwork.

But seriously, these comic strips and memes would not exist if there wasn't a reason for them. When group work is not structured properly, a variety of problems arise including

- groupthink
- hitchhiking
- one member doing most of the work
- superficial conversation
- group grades that over-reward some while penalizing others
- dominating members
- invisible members.

The way we set up group work can determine its success. Here are a few basics to consider:

Begin by thinking about the learning task: Does it lend itself to collaboration?

- If the task does not require collaboration for completion, then it should be completed by students individually.

- If the task requires collaboration, use the smallest-sized group necessary. If pairs can complete the task, use pairs.

- Use a larger group of three or four when the academic task requires more diverse thinking and background knowledge (see Figure 4.34).

- The larger the group, the longer it will take to complete the task. If you are short on time, use pairs.

- It's best to avoid groups larger than four when possible: it takes sophisticated collaboration skills

Figure 4.34 **These members are responding to a poem—and to one another's written responses. Here a group of four is advantageous because it offers diverse insight and background knowledge.**

to keep all members of larger groups equally engaged. As the group gets larger, it becomes more likely that some members will dominate while others will disengage or hitchhike, allowing other members to complete the bulk of the work. When should you use a group larger than four? When you are working with students who have attendance issues. Larger groups are necessary when on any given day, groups are actually whittled down to four because of that day's absences.

Whenever groups meet, explicitly state the collaborative skill expectations.

You might say, "As you work today, I'm going to be listening in, sitting in, and monitoring for skills that will help you achieve the academic task as well as make the time spent together enjoyable and fun. Here's what I'm looking for." And then post the target behaviors where students can see them throughout their meeting. These expectations might include

1. using quiet voices
2. using the text

3. encouraging even participation

4. asking follow-up questions

5. offering friendliness and support to all members (see Reinforce Friendliness and Support, page 92)

6. focusing solely on group members.

Try to aim for no more than six explicit behaviors; more than that becomes overwhelming. Then, as students work collaboratively, roam the room listening in on discussion and observing which behaviors are in use and which ones are forgotten. When you notice low use of a stated skill, it's okay to intervene in a group and say, "I've noticed you've forgotten to use skill number 5. Take a look at the skill list right now and think of a friendliness and support statement you could say to the group right now." Offer some wait time and then continue. "Before I leave, take turns giving others in your group some friendliness and support." Listen to the statements, congratulate the group on their use of the skill, remind them to keep using it even when you aren't present, and then move on to the next group. Of course, it's highly likely that these skill statements will sound a little stilted, at least initially, but that's okay. Skill integration is progressive. As explained in Chapter 2 (see page 53), learning a new collaborative skill moves through four predictable steps: reluctance, awkwardness, overuse, integration.

Have students come to group work prepared with their own individual work.

Depending on your students, this preparation for the group meeting may be completed in class or for homework, but it's important that students do not join the group empty-handed (see Figure 4.35). Coming prepared greatly increases the likelihood that groups will have engaging, on-topic discussions while greatly decreasing the likelihood of hitchhikers.

Figure 4.35 **When students read and prepare notes individually before group work, the group discussion is far more likely to be deep and thought-provoking while also avoiding "groupthink."**

Figure 4.36 Even though this memorized performance of a scene from *Othello* counted as part of their final exam grade, these sophomore students self-evaluated their contributions to the group during practice and then evaluated their performance when they watched the video. No group grades were assigned.

Avoid giving group grades.

Group grades are the number one way to get your students to hate working together. Instead, give students opportunities to self-evaluate (see page 154), recognizing their contributions to the group as well as their improvement goals (see Figure 4.36).

Avoid complicated group projects—at least at first.

While group projects can teach students how to recognize individual member talents and strengths, divide work evenly and keep all members accountable; pushing complicated projects upon student groups too early will guarantee disaster for some of your students. And even in group projects, have students evaluate themselves individually rather than assigning one big group grade.

MOVE>Heighten Students' Understanding of Their Own Collaboration Skills

Immediate Result: Group members gain better awareness of their use of collaboration skills.

Long-Term Result: Students increase and refine their use of these skills, using them automatically, without prompting.

Giving kids frequent opportunities to work together is essential in building their collaboration skills. However, it's not all they need to become supportive, productive collaborators. They also need to refine their collaboration skills—something they'll be more motivated to do if they can see tangible improvements in their discussions.

A good way to start the conversation about skills is by asking students to list the skills necessary for productive small-group work. Your students' suggestions might include the following:

- using quiet voices
- directing the group's work
- keeping the group on task
- connecting personal feelings, reactions, and experiences to the text
- paraphrasing
- using the text to support an idea
- being friendly and supportive
- recognizing good ideas
- energizing the group

- disagreeing with ideas respectfully

- asking follow-up questions

- using names

- taking turns leading the discussion

- encouraging the participation of others

- giving in-depth answers

- adding on to another's idea (piggybacking).

Once the class has brainstormed a list, let students identify six or seven skills that they think would be most important for them to work on. Then create a self-observation chart with those skills (see Figure 4.37). Before a group meets for discussion, pass out a copy of the chart to each student, asking them to review the skills listed and circle three that they personally want to work on. The members do not need to negotiate skills: the skill decision is entirely up to each individual student. Then, as the groups meet for discussion, each member should do their best to keep track of when they use one of those three skills by putting a check or a tick mark in the box below that skill. After the discussion, have students replay their own participation in their heads and write down specific things they said or did that reflected any of the three skills they were focusing on. Once they've thought on their own, it's fine for the group members to talk together about the skills, sharing their discussion memories with one another so that each member might get a few more examples of their own personal skill usage. Finally, have students reflect individually on the data they've recorded and determine a skill goal they want to aim for in their next discussion. This might include trying to improve their use of the skills they focused on in the just-concluded discussion, or it might mean choosing some new skills to work on.

As students work in their groups, monitor their conversations and their skill usage. Typically, you will find that when groups really get into a discussion, they forget all about their self-observation, so it's okay to break in for a moment and remind them to keep track of their collaborative skills. And when you do intervene, start by describing some of the skills you saw students use: "Joe, that was an excellent follow-up question you asked Susan just now. And Susan, you did a great job going back to that page in

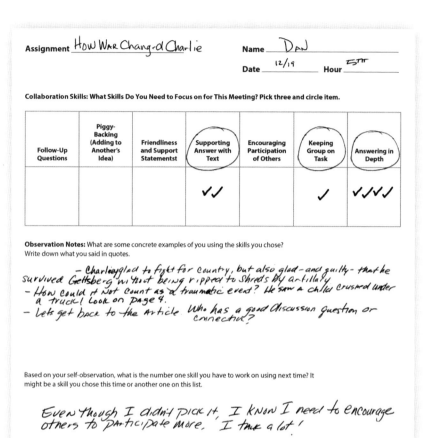

Assignment __How War Changed Charlie__   Name __Dan__
                                                Date __12/19__   Hour __5th__

Collaboration Skills: What Skills Do You Need to Focus on for This Meeting? Pick three and circle item.

Follow-Up Questions	Piggy-Backing (Adding to Another's Idea)	Friendliness and Support Statementst	Supporting Answer with Text	Encouraging Participation of Others	Keeping Group on Task	Answering in Depth
			✓✓		✓	✓✓✓

Observation Notes: What are some concrete examples of you using the skills you chose?
Write down what you said in quotes.

- Charlie glad to fight for country, but also glad - and guilty - that he survived Gettsberg without being ripped to shreds by artillary
- How could it not count as a traumatic event? He saw a child crushed under a truck! Look on page 4.
- Lets get back to the Article. Who has a good discussion question or connection?

Based on your self-observation, what is the number one skill you have to work on using next time? It might be a skill you chose this time or another one on this list.

Even though I didn't pick it, I know I need to encourage others to participate more. I talk a lot!

Figure 4.37 **This sample self-observation form shows improved small-group performance because of heightened awareness of the necessary discussion and collaboration skills.**

the book and showing everyone how you drew that conclusion. Tom and Karen, you both did a great job following along in the book as well as listening carefully to what Susan was saying. Before I leave, I just want to remind you to keep track of your skills on the self-observation sheet. So far, it looks like you've used hardly any skills at all, but watching you just now makes me think you're forgetting to record your skills. Keep up the good work! I'll stop by again a little later and see how you're doing!"

MOVE>Guide Students in Academic Self-Evaluation and Goal Setting

Immediate Result: Students use criteria to analyze their own work.

Long-Term Result: Students begin to see their own growth as they track feedback as a tangible record of growth and accomplishment

Thanks to grading criteria that overwhelmingly focus on points and online grading systems that give students, parents, and guardians 24/7 online access to grades, it can be easy for students (and adults) to forget the real purpose of assignments: learning! Therefore, we need to help students, parents, and guardians focus on tangible academic successes. One way to do this is to show students how to keep a record of their goals and accomplishments in regard to predictable types of assignments. In English language arts, for example, the focus might be writing (see Figures 4.38 and 4.39). In science, it might be lab reports.

WRITING RECORD				
Writing Assignment	Grade	Strengths	Growth Opportunities	Goal for Next Time

Figure 4.38 Sheila Furey Sullivan made this form for her ninth-grade English students. While this form focuses on writing assignments, the same structure can be used to help students track their progress in any subject.

WRITING RECORD				
Writing Assignment	Grade	Strengths	Growth Opportunities	Goal for Next Time
Theme diorama	42/50 points 84%	Good start	Don't read off the paper. Develop more support.	Work on my weakness and explain the theme a little better next time.
Roger body paragraph	19/20 points 95%	Explained well, clearly stated and written well.	Fix convention errors a(n), has/had. Work on reading ins and outs.	I will try to keep up the good work and fix my errors on conventions, attention getters, and transitions.
Book Review	83/90 points 92%	Good job citing quotes and explaining certain quotes. Good tie-in used in the conclusion.	Work on the awkward wording. Need to work on the pronunciation. Reread and rework on grammar errors.	I'll try to change up my wording and make it less confusing to read and to work on the convention errors I made.
Immigration argument essay	77/90 points 85%	Format. Points stated from strongest to weakest.	Unclear analysis and wording. Very bad citing work. Read over work for confusing, unclear thoughts. Didn't make time to visit writing center.	GO TO THE CENTER!! And also learn to fix citations. State all sources.

Figure 4.39 **Keeping an ongoing record of strengths, weaknesses, and goals from one assignment to the next enabled this student to review their previous reflections in order to improve their work and follow through on previous goals as they complete the major writing assignments English 9. There is no doubt that this student will be visiting the writing center as they work on their next paper!**

Begin to plan for student self-evaluation before the kids ever walk into your classroom by determining how they will archive their work. It might be by using a binder or, depending on the technology available, by using an online option such as Google Docs. Either way, this needs to be a living, breathing work archive where students regularly add pieces as well as compare their completed artifacts, noticing how they've progressed and also where there is potential for growth.

While grades are a requirement of most school environments, grades are also very abstract and hold very little specific information. Other than the facts that a grade of C is two grades away from an A and is often equated with a descriptor of "average," what does a C tell you about a student's skills? Not much. In comparison, when students analyze their work, they can learn to spot patterns, strengths, and weaknesses. And, once they become experts in their own work, they have a better idea of how to improve that work. Plus, for students who often lose track of finished assignments, frequent self-reflection gives them a necessary reason to keep their work. Finally, the process of analyzing their work gives you opportunities to teach them ways to be organized and accountable for their own progress.

Time for Action!

This chapter includes many options so that you'll always have a move ready when you need it. Threading these classroom strategies and activities through the school year, alongside and intertwined with content-area teaching, will keep your classroom community strong.

While these moves will take only a few minutes each day, we all know that classroom time is precious. If you find that your concerns about time are keeping you from tending to the classroom community, consider where you could be saving time. The best way to find the time necessary for relationship building is by eliminating activities and practices that offer little return on investment. For example, isolated grammar instruction has no correlation with improved writing skills (Hillocks and Smith 1991). Why continue to do it? Take a careful look at your daily agendas and scrutinize the activities in regard to their usefulness in students skill building and learning. Then pitch the ones that take up time yet offer little learning value.

Because responding to students in writing is part of relationship and community building (as in the letter writing activity on page 108), we teachers also need to reconsider how we're using our time outside class. One way to find the time to correspond with your students is to hand over the role of primary paper grader and assessor to your students. Just as people are far more interested and invested in those they know and have positive feelings about, people are also far more interested and invested in changing, improving, and refining their skills when they are the ones collecting the data and setting the goals. By turning assessment over to our students while guiding them in their reflections, we are helping them grow as learners. Therefore, as you take action, do think about the ways you can offer students increased opportunity to conduct their own assessments.

How's It Going?

This checklist is divided into questions that roughly reflect the three areas this chapter addresses. Check off the ones that you can answer yes to, and your responses will give you some feedback on what you might want to return to or attend to.

EXPAND ACQUAINTANCESHIP

☐ Have you eliminated time-consuming, unrewarding grading practices that, upon reflection, produce little academic or interpersonal growth for your students?

☐ Have students written you a letter of introduction? Have you found the time to write back? If not, return to and reconsider the previous question.

☐ As you read and responded to student letters of introduction, did you simultaneously collect interesting details that could be funneled into a "Find Someone Who" activity?

☐ Has student–teacher conferring moved beyond those quick doorway chats at the beginning and end of the period? If so, have you worked with students to troubleshoot conferring roadblocks and develop valuable work that students can complete quietly and individually during conference time? (Developing a system of conferring that takes place in a regular, predictable way will take some time. Many teachers start out with high hopes but quickly drop the practice because of management issues. The only way to resolve the issue is to work with students to create solutions.)

☐ Do students know the names of all their classmates and pronounce those names correctly?

☐ Are students changing partners or work groups regularly so that by the end of the year or semester they will have worked with all their classmates?

VALUE AND APPRECIATE CLASSMATES

☐ Have students had the chance to investigate their own family's hidden talents via Funds of Knowledge maps and then had the chance to share their discoveries with classmates?

- [ ] Do student work groups regularly explore the interests and experiences they have in common?

- [ ] When students work together, does the meeting end with an opportunity to acknowledge the specific contributions of each member?

- [ ] Is the whole class celebrating accomplishments—academic and interpersonal—of individuals, groups, and the entire class on a regular basis?

STRENGTHEN STUDENT ACCOUNTABILITY

- [ ] Do student group members complete individual work prior to a discussion in order to prevent hitchhiking and groupthink?

- [ ] Are you carefully structuring small-group tasks for success, using pairs whenever feasible and explicitly teaching or reviewing the interpersonal skills necessary for the assignment?

- [ ] Are alternative assessments to group grades always used? (Reminder: the quickest way to sour students on collaborative work is to assign group grades.)

- [ ] Are students learning to accurately self-assess their interpersonal work and academic work? Is assessment a task equally owned by the students and teacher?

Wow, that was a lot, wasn't it? Pat yourself on the back for whatever you checked off. The key now is to keep doing the items you checked off while adding something else to try. If you've run into a classroom management snag, quite a few of the lessons in this chapter will help you get that classroom community moving forward again after a temporary derailment. You'll find further help for diffusing disruptions in the next chapter.

5

Staying the Course

All of us have at least one clear memory of a moment when things went wrong in our classroom. It's a visceral memory, a nearly physical sensation that the ground is rapidly shifting. It might be a time when a disagreement in class turned into a showdown, a time when someone yelled angrily, or a time when you feared that the class might rise up like an angry mob.

It's in moments like these that we might find ourselves reverting back to traditional classroom management methods: giving detentions, sending kids to the principal's office, or becoming defensive and authoritarian in the face of a confrontation. In my early years of teaching, I did those things, too. Our own panic, embarrassment, or anger can make it feel as though we must assert our authority and impose order immediately. But the cost of this kind of reaction is high: it erodes community, weakens our relationships with our students, and shows students that their compliance—not their education or their happiness—is our highest priority. As a result, it becomes more and more necessary to actively motivate and police students each day—all of which takes the class' emphasis off learning.

Instead of reverting back to traditional attempts to maintain control, we can continue to rely on the same principles that we've used in previous chapters: friendliness, support, and community. These are far more powerful tools than detentions and punishments: they head off many disruptions before they happen; they lessen the frequency and intensity of the remaining disruptions; they provide powerful and long-lasting options for resolving disruptions; and they model the same behaviors we want to encourage in our students.

How Can Friendliness, Support, and Community Help Us Resolve Conflicts?

Let's take a look at how three different teachers collaborated with their students to avert and diffuse classroom disruptions.

Sixth-grade teacher Anna Dunlap recalls a student who became inattentive and overactive at different times of the day. Anna learned from the student and his family that he had type 1 diabetes and that his distracted (and distracting) behavior coincided with times when his blood sugar was high. Rather than punishing the student for misbehavior, Anna came up with a solution based on supporting the student. As she explains:

> Instead of calling him out each afternoon, we developed a hand signal that was very discreet. I would tap my thumb and middle finger together so he could see it, and that's when he knew to check his blood sugar. He would pull out his monitor and check it there at his table. He would then calculate his units and give himself insulin. This would all happen without ever having to stop class. The other students at his table barely even noticed this was all happening.

Lindsey Jones, a seventh-grade English teacher, remembers Anthony, a former student diagnosed with obsessive-compulsive disorder (OCD). At the beginning of the school year, Lindsey took time to speak with Anthony about what would make him comfortable in class: she learned that he had a great deal of anxiety about germs and that he would prefer to have his own desk, rather than share a table with other students. Lindsey took pride in her classroom community and the table seating that promoted collaboration. However, she knew that Anthony needed an environment he could depend on from day to day to truly be at ease in the class—his own desk, where he could arrange his materials as he wished and, when he thought it necessary, sanitize with alcohol wipes.

Group work often made Anthony very anxious, so Lindsey gave him the option to work alone. But there was one boy in the class who was exceptionally patient, empathetic, and socially skilled. Lindsey recognized this student's kindness and encouraged him to be Anthony's link to the rest of the class. When students formed groups, he always stopped by Anthony's desk first and asked him if he'd like a partner. Usually Anthony said no, but sometimes he said yes. At the end of the year, Anthony's mother thanked Lindsey for the strides Anthony had made and for making English Anthony's favorite class.

Ryan was a sophomore English student of mine. He wasn't one to mouth off in class, but he had a long-practiced habit of not doing schoolwork. As August ran into September, I concluded that he had the literacy skills to succeed, but he still wasn't doing much work. As a result, he was failing the class. Around this time my students began participating in writing circles: each group agrees on a topic, writes about it in whatever way they wish, and then reads aloud what they wrote to their group the following day (Vopat 2009). Students' feedback focuses on telling the writer about the things they liked in the piece. Ryan enjoyed sharing his pieces with his group, but often showed up empty-handed. Now, my compliance-style gut reaction would have been to tell Ryan that without a piece, he couldn't join the group. However, if I did that, I might have squashed what little forward movement Ryan had made regarding schoolwork. (Remember, at the beginning of the year he did nothing.) So instead, I said, "Ryan, it looks like you've come to the group without any writing. I worry that without anything to share you'll be bored. Is that going to be a problem?" Ryan responded that he enjoyed listening to his members' pieces and he would have something written the next time. I took him at his word and moved on to observe other groups. When I did get back to Ryan's group, he was listening, enjoying the writing, and generously offering great positive comments to his group members' pieces. Gradually, Ryan came prepared more and more often. As he was finding schoolwork more rewarding because of the interaction, his homework habits began to improve.

Fast-forward to fourth quarter. Ryan managed to pass each quarter. Performing scenes from *Othello* was the final project of the year. Working in a duet scene, Ryan turned out to have a sense for acting and blocking. He and his partner had their lines perfectly memorized and interpreted. Their blocking and costumes were great—so great that their scene became *the* recorded scene I showed the following year's classes when I wanted them to understand what a superb scene looked like.

Proactively Defusing and Productively Resolving Conflicts

You've no doubt noticed that none of these stories include a dramatic classroom management crisis—there is no yelling, no slamming of doors, no students causing each other emotional turmoil. That's because Anna, Lindsey, and I headed those possibilities off at the pass by being responsive to our students before there was a serious issue. We focused on supporting our students rather than trying to control them. Consider how things might have unfolded if we'd taken more traditional approaches: any one of those situations could have become tense and difficult over the course of the year if we'd demanded compliance. Instead, all three students had positive outcomes and there were no in-class showdowns.

The moves in this chapter aim to keep you and your class on track for a good year by keeping energy high, by strengthening your alliances with students' families, and by dealing with issues productively when they arise. All the lessons and ideas presented in this chapter reflect the idea of working *with* students, helping them make good decisions, and finding solutions that enable them to feel empowered and in control of their lives. To help students, we need to listen to them, we need to empathize, and we have to give up once and for all the notion that when it comes to class rules "one size fits all." Each student is their own individual and we need to meet them on their terms. And part of meeting the needs of all students means letting them and their parents and guardians know early and often that their good work has offered us joy. Even when students behave in ways that we find disappointing, our goal as teachers is not to mete out punishment but to help students think about their behavior in ways that enable them to make better choices the next time.

GOAL	MOVES
Re-energize the Work	• Start a New Semester or Grading Period on a Positive Word (page 166) • Practice Mental Focus Through Centering (page 168) • Teach Students How to Address Issues in Class (page 171) • Solve Class Problems Together (page 175)
Bolster Alliances	• Observe a Success and Document It in a Positive Note (page 181) • Turn Conference Night into a Conversation About Learning (page 186) • Create Partnerships When Communicating with Parents and Guardians (Even During Tough Conversations) (page 189)
Get Back on Track	• Address Issues Without Escalating the Situation (page 199) • Invite Students to Document Their Behavior (page 206) • Confer with Students to Help Them Recognize and Revise Ineffective Behavior (page 208) • Keep a Record of Your Problem-Solving (page 213) • Use a Proactive Approach with Supervisors, Deans, Principals, and Guidance Counselors (page 216)

Goal: Re-energize the Work

Lessons to support this goal:

- Start a New Semester or Grading Period on a Positive Word (page 166)
- Practice Mental Focus Through Centering (page 168)
- Teach Students How to Address Issues in Class (page 171)
- Solve Class Problems Together (page 175)

TRADITIONAL APPROACH	COLLABORATIVE APPROACH
• Learning goals mainly come from the syllabus. • Students are told to "leave their baggage at the door." • The teacher owns all the problems in class and is solely responsible for the solutions.	• Learners are given the opportunity to share their goals. • Students are directly taught how to center their thinking before diving into academic tasks. • Problem-solving is addressed by the classroom community.
⬇ LEADS TO ⬇	⬇ LEADS TO ⬇
∅ Students feel disconnected from the teacher, the other students, and from learning. ∅ Students have little ownership (and, therefore, little interest) in classroom problem-solving or self-control since it is the teacher who is in charge and makes unilateral decisions without their input. ∅ Any sense of order in the classroom comes from the teacher, in the form of attempts to "control" students using punishments or rewards. Because students have no reason to be invested in the classroom community, the punishment or reward system needs to be constant to be effective.	✔ Learners know their voice and ideas are important. ✔ Students recognize and take ownership of their role in creating an atmosphere for learning.

Figure 5.1

MOVE> Start a New Semester or Grading Period on a Positive Word

Immediate Result: Students see that their goals are a priority for you and that your class is a place where they matter.

Long-Term Result: Students track their progress against a goal that is meaningful to them, giving them opportunities to be introspective and to make changes. Additionally, they understand that their goals (and, therefore, they) are respected by you, the teacher.

How we begin a quarter or semester sends a message about what is most important in a classroom. Launching into an explanation of the content to be covered, for example, tells students that the content is the most important factor in the class. Instead, we can learn from how seventh-grade English teacher Andrea Arndt begins a new term.

Andrea likes to begin the semester on a positive note. On the first day back to class after winter break, she has each student think about a word that will inspire them, asking, "What's a word that reflects something you want to accomplish in the upcoming months?" She starts by modeling her own word and brief explanation of why she chose it (see Figure 5.2). The emphasis is on choosing a word that reflects an intentional and attainable goal. However, the word does not need to be academically or content-area oriented. Andrea also emphasizes that these words will be shared: a public commitment often means that you're a little bit more

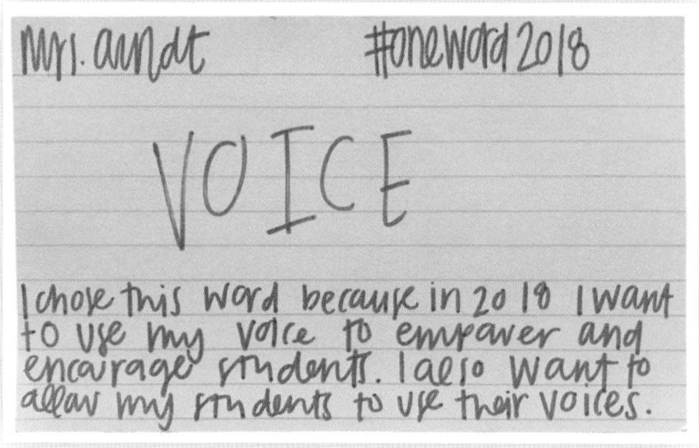

Mrs. arndt   #oneword 2018

VOICE

I chose this word because in 2018 I want to use my voice to empower and encourage students. I also want to allow my students to use their voices.

Figure 5.2 **Andrea Arndt starts her students' #oneword goal thinking by displaying her own word.**

likely to achieve a goal. Plus, everyone else in class is here to help one another when the going gets a little rough! After answering any questions, Andrea gives students time to think, talk together, and personally arrive upon the word that best reflects a goal they would like to aim for (see Figure 5.3). Once everyone has created a card, Andrea posts them on a wall and invites students to visit these words for insight into and inspiration from

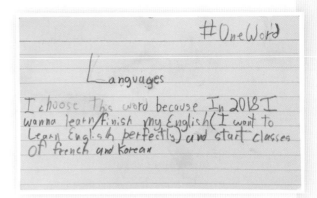

Figure 5.3 **Students choose the word that best fits them for the upcoming semester. Their words do not need to be directly connected with a subject or school.**

their classmates (see Figure 5.4). Students revisit their words after school holidays and write briefly about their word, what it has meant to them so far, and how they are going to use it to motivate and inspire them for the rest of the year. At the end of the term, Andrea lets them take their note cards. "Some students may very well throw the cards out as soon as they leave my room," she says, "but I would like to think they keep them!"

Figure 5.4 **Students are invited to revisit these goals before the bell rings and during the last few minutes of class. Andrea finds that her students are more likely to meet their goals when they are encouraged to visit the display with classmates and given time to talk together about how they are doing.**

MOVE>Practice Mental Focus Through Centering

> **Immediate Result:** Students focus on the moment rather than the thoughts and memories that make up so much of our brain chatter.
>
> **Long-Term Result:** As students begin to understand the power of centering, it becomes a tool they can use independently, empowering them as they understand how to have greater self-control.

Seeing his fourth graders buffeted by the everyday trials of life and by even more trying circumstances, science teacher Mitch Lazarus began to look for something that would enable his students to better focus as well as self-regulate. Inspired by the book *The Biology of Belief* by Bruce H. Lipton, Mitch developed the following centering routine:

1. Close your eyes and take three slow, deep breaths in and out.

2. Begin saying an unimportant word or sound in your head such as *is* or *ah*. Centering works best if you pick a word that on its own has little meaning, because the meaning can distract you.

3. While you are focusing on your word or sound, notice when you receive any other thoughts; notice what's "yelling" at you inside your head. Instead of shifting your focus, brush these thoughts away by mentally saying, "Pass on by." Then return to your word and continue centering until the time is up (Mitch found that centering for 60 to 90 seconds works best).

After about a minute of centering, Mitch brings his students back to the moment and the work at hand. Students report feeling refreshed, energized, positively focused, and ready to get busy (see Figure 5.5). Centering enables students to let go of the argument they had with a parent, guardian, or friend once they recognize that replaying the incident over and over in their head only negatively affects the present experience or interaction.

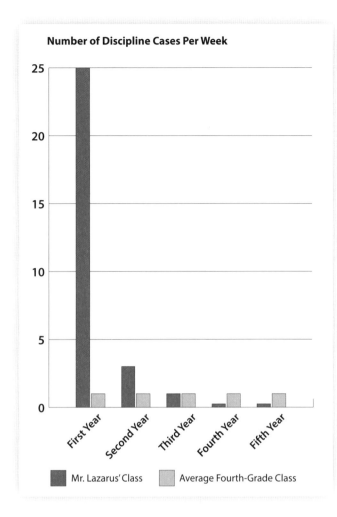

Number of Discipline Cases Per Week

Mr. Lazarus' Class ▪ Average Fourth-Grade Class

Figure 5.5 **Mitch Lazarus' first-year teaching inexperience and classroom management problems led him to begin experimenting with centering. Being a science teacher, he automatically incorporated some action research to see if how he worked with students changed their behaviors. It did! When Mitch's role expanded to working with grades 4–8, he found that centering was equally effective at different grade levels.**

While research is ongoing, the positive effects of mindfulness are being documented in a wide array of fields. Professional football and baseball teams are beginning to offer their players mindfulness training (Braff 2019), as is the U.S. military. According to a 2018 study published in *Progress in Brain Research* (Zanesco et al. 2018) reported:

> *The 4-week mindfulness training (MT) group significantly improved over time on attention and working memory outcome measures . . . Together, these results suggest that short-form MT, when delivered over a 4-week delivery schedule, may be an effective cognitive training tool in elite military cohorts.*

Thomas Armstrong, in his 2019 book *Mindfulness in the Classroom*, writes that mindfulness practices result in neuroplastic changes in the brain. Mindfulness appears to reduce connectivity between regions of the brain that drive stress while strengthening connectivity between regions of the brain that enable greater focus, concentration, and calmness (Armstrong 2019).

While these new studies are establishing a neuroscience foundation for why the practice of mindfulness offers improved thinking and self-regulation, mindfulness trials from 2012 and 2014, reviewed by the National Center for Complementary and Integrative Health, a branch of the National Institute of Health (NIH), show moderate effectiveness in reducing anxiety and depression (2016). Ongoing research at the University of Chicago Crime Lab is examining "whether a meditation program offers tangible benefits for teens at Gage Park High School where 98.3 percent of the students are considered low income." One student from the program reported in an interview that although he had been quick to anger and often was arguing and fighting, he felt calmer as a result of the meditation program. He now thinks about how to react when someone says something objectionable or when he finds himself in a stressful interaction (O'Connell 2017). It's interesting to note that this high school student's observations about his own self-regulation are very similar to what Mitch's fourth-grade students reported.

MOVE>Teach Students How to Address Issues in Class

Immediate Result: In-class interactions are improved.

Long-Term Result: Students feel heard, honored, and empowered as they take the lead in improving in-class interactions. Mastering additional skills enables students to work more productively together as well as achieve more academically due to decreased distraction and increased cooperation.

As teachers, if we notice that our students are not engaged or that they're not having productive conversations in class, we often feel the need to jump in and tell them what to do: we say, "Pay attention!" or "Be sure to listen to the others in your group." Yet we all know that reminders like these rarely have a lasting effect. Furthermore, when they're repeated as often as we seem to think necessary, students begin to hear them not as helpful reminders but as nagging. The solution? Let the students solve the problem instead.

To do this, we'll use a teaching move first introduced in Chapter 3, Teach Collaborative Skills Directly. In that move, the teacher introduced the skill—friendliness and support—that the class would be defining by creating a T-chart. In this current move, the students will once again define a necessary skill using a T-chart but they will also take the responsibility of identifying the skill(s) the class needs to function more smoothly and collaborate more effectively.

Why ask the students to identify the skills the class needs to emphasize? First, they're the experts. Just as you, as a participant at the occasional (or not-so-occasional) dysfunctional faculty meeting, can easily spot how the meeting might be improved, your students, who are part of this class every day, can see what needs to be fine-tuned. Second, putting this responsibility in students' hands helps them see how they have the power to make positive changes. Finally, all of us are more likely to work toward the success of ideas that we had a hand in shaping.

Begin by sharing a list of skills like the one below with your students.

Maintenance Skills	Academic Skills
Using quiet voices	Asking questions
Forming groups quickly	Asking follow-up questions
Staying on task	Summarizing
Appreciating contributions	Asking for help
Taking turns	Giving help
Encouraging participation	Checking for understanding
Offering friendliness and support	Developing consensus
Being respectful	Disagreeing agreeably
Being responsible	Supporting ideas with text
Rising above	Connecting content ideas or information

Ask students which skill would most enhance their small-group work and conversations. It may be that students choose a skill that wouldn't have been your top pick. Trust them and go with their choice: they know what is hampering them better than we do. Once your class has agreed on the most important skill to add to their repertoire, use the "Looks Like"/"Sounds Like" structure students learned in Chapter 3 (page 82):

1. Start by asking students how their group work might change if every member were using this skill. You might even have students write about it for a minute before they share some ideas in the large group.

2. Next, have pairs brainstorm on a T-chart (see Figure 5.6 and Online Reference 5.1) what group members would look like and what group members would be saying if they were using that skill.

3. Finally, return to the large group and create a master T-chart, taking suggestions from all the pairs.

Looks Like	Sounds Like

Figure 5.6 **The T-chart is a useful tool for explicitly defining important, positive behaviors. Don't neglect filling out the "Looks Like" column. Though the required body language is similar no matter what the skill, students need regular reminding that our actions and our words need to match the intended message.**

The Power of "Looks Like"/"Sounds Like"

"Looks Like"/"Sounds Like" charts turn intangible goals (like "getting along") into doable actions. Each time we use a "Looks Like"/"Sounds Like" chart to translate good intentions into achievable, specific, everyday behaviors, we illustrate for students that they have the power to make big changes.

Now, the real work begins: incorporating the newly identified behaviors into group discussions. While the creation of a T-chart and subsequent skill incorporation might have been new to your students when the principle of friendliness and support was introduced, this time you can turn the implementation question back to the students: "Now that we have this great T-chart, how are we going to make sure we actually use this important skill?" This question could be part of another large-group brainstorming session, or you can let each individual group come up with its own plan and then share it with the class. After groups work together, set aside time for them to reflect on

Rise Above
you said it...

LOOKS LIKE	SOUNDS LIKE
• Writing/reading more than the minimum	• "Do you want help with...?"
• Stepping up to do something when no one else does	• "I'll go first."
• Helping teammates	• "I stand firm in my belief that..."
• Studying, reviewing notes	• "We need to be doing this."
• Going to a teacher if you see bullying	• "Maybe we should add more."
• Leading a small group	• "We are supposed to be..."
• Good grades	• "Can I write more...?"
• Taking a stand for what's right	• "Please, tell me more about that."
• Confidence in yourself	• "Don't be mean."
	• "I refuse to follow the crowd."
	• "Since I finished early, I could..."
	• "I've got this."
	• "Mrs. Jones, I know about a situation that needs attention from an adult."

the skills they have been trying to master, discussing specific implementation examples as well as how they can use the skill better the next time they meet (see Figures 5.7, 5.8, and 5.9). The self-observation form example discussed in the move Heighten Students' Understanding of Their Own Collaboration Skills (Figure 4.37 on page 153) is also an excellent way to help students remember to use skills they are working to master.

Be respectful.
you said it...

LOOKS like	SOUNDS like
• Following directions	• Silence (during independent work or when someone has the floor)
• Assisting a classmate	• "Hey, guys, let's pay attention."
• Raising your hand for help	• "Yes, ma'am."
• Sitting up, looking at speaker	• "Thank you" and "You're welcome"
• Taking care of books and materials	• "Please"
• Keeping hands to self	• "That's a good idea."
• On task (pencil moving, sitting at assigned seat, etc.)	• "I'll share first."
	• "I'd like to hear what you thought."
	• "I really like how you..."

Be Responsible.
you said it...

looks like	Sounds like
• Arriving to class on time	• Having a response if your stick is drawn
• Staying on task	• Having a presentation down
• Keeping up with work	• "First, we need to..."
• Turning work into trays ON TIME	• "Let's listen to what ___ has to say."
• Cleaning up your area (supplies back in box, personal belongings gathered, throw trash away)	• "I'm sorry for..."
• Using class time wisely (always doing something)	• "Wait...what? Can you explain that again?"
• Bringing book + journal daily	• "I need help with..."
• Following directions	• "I will share first."
• Books open, pencils moving	• "I got my paper signed."
	• "Let me help you."
	• "I have lost ___. Where can I get another one?"
	• "I think it would be a good idea if we..."

Figure 5.7, Figure 5.8, and Figure 5.9
Lindsey Jones' eighth graders focused on maintenance behaviors that enabled them to work together more productively, both as a whole class and in individual small groups.

MOVE>Solve Class Problems Together

> **Immediate Result:** The problem in your classroom is owned and solved by all the stakeholders.
>
> **Long-Term Result:** Students learn that problems within the classroom community are problems that can be solved only by the community. As a result, students will become better at dealing with academic and behavioral problems in positive, successful ways, rather than avoiding the problem and allowing frustration, resentment, and blaming to simmer. Plus, for you as the teacher, it is freeing to know that you are not the only one in the classroom responsible for solving problems as they arise.

When teachers and students work together and attempt to collaborate, issues—both academic and behavioral—will arise. Unfortunately, we teachers often react immediately with this question: "How can I solve this problem and get this situation back under my control?" Instead, we need to replace that question with this one: "What triggers this problem and what can we do to solve it together?" Lots of times just putting a problem out on the table for discussion diminishes its power and brings a resolution closer. More importantly, by working through the issue with your students, you're demonstrating that you do not have all the answers and that you do respect their thinking, experience, and insight. You're sending the message that what affects one of us affects all of us. Offering students regular opportunities to solve problems as they arise encourages creative thinking, shared power, and greater investment in the solution—all of which make it more likely that students will improve their abilities of self-regulation and self-advocacy.

Get started by describing the problem and asking students to think about what triggers the problem. Here's an example of what that might sound like:

> I've noticed that quite a few people in class have a hard time getting settled down and ready to work at the beginning of the hour. Lots of side conversations continue when I try to get everyone's attention, and many of you are very slow to get the necessary supplies out. Sometimes it takes up to 5 minutes to get going—that's a lot of time when you consider that we only have 42 minutes together each day. What do you think are the reasons why many of you are slow to settle down? Think about this question and jot down the reasons.

Give students a few minutes to write and a minute to share with their partners. Then have partners rank their reasons. Lead a quick large-group share, with each pair stating their number one reason for the problem. After hearing a reason, the rest of the class should give a quick thumbs-up if that reason occurred in their top three. Now pose the second question, which positions students as having useful expertise:

> While I'm busy teaching in this room most of the day, you have the chance to observe lots of other teachers. I want you to take the role of educational experts. I'm certain we aren't the only class that's ever encountered this problem. Using your past experiences in other classrooms, how have other teachers solved this problem? Think about the circumstances that trigger this problem and the possible solutions we could try. Think and write for a few minutes.

Give students a few minutes to write, and then continue:

> I bet that as education experts you can come up with some possible solutions to the problem that might work for us even better than anything any of your teachers have tried. Think about that and see if you can generate an even better solution to the problem.

Give students a few more minutes to think and write. Follow with this instruction to partners:

> Get together with your partner and share all the ideas you have for solving this problem. After you share, I want you to pick the best solution among all your ideas. Here's the definition of best solution: the solution you think would positively solve

the problem and work best for everyone. What solution could everyone buy into
and work toward together?

As students are finishing up their solution choices, ask for a volunteer to write down the best ideas on the board, on a piece of paper under a doc cam, or on a projected computer screen. Lead another quick large-group share, with each pair stating its best solution to the problem. After hearing from all the pairs, take a look at the board. If there are any possible solutions that won't work for you, cross them out and explain why.

I guess you're right that the talking and getting down to work wouldn't be a
problem if every day were a free day, but I'm charged by the administration to
teach and help you progress in your learning of this subject, so that's a solution I'm
going to have to cross off our list since it would be against school policy. Even so,
I see a lot of other possibilities here that could work. Which one do you think we
should try?

Go through the list and get a quick thumbs-up vote for each solution. Pick one that was popular with students but also will work for you. Sometimes, students will tell you to just kick the disruptive students out of class, probably because this is what they have seen other teachers do on many occasions. If this occurs, here's a response:

I'm really uncomfortable with that solution. You may have seen it used in other
classrooms, but it makes me feel like a sheriff more than a teacher and it feels like it
puts you and me on different teams. What's a solution that would involve all of us,
each trying to contribute something positive that would help all of us?

Agree on a solution that everyone in the class can abide by, and conclude:

I think this solution has some potential. And you know what, maybe the first
solution won't work, and we'll have to try something else. The important thing is
that we keep working together to find a solution. That's the way life works whether
you're in school, at work, or at home with your family!

Giving students power in this process helps make the resolution that you land upon be something that they are invested in. It's worth the time it takes. However, if you're concerned that a process this open-ended won't be productive in a particular instance, you can shorten up this lesson: Divide the problem-solving into two parts. Once pairs have picked their best solution, collect the papers and assure students that one of their ideas will be implemented the following day. Collecting the papers gives you the chance to see what they've written. Instead of making a complete in-class list, pick the three or four ideas you think will work best for everyone, and put those ideas up on the board for the class to choose from using the same thumbs-up voting described earlier.

When offered the opportunity, students will take responsibility and offer solutions that enable them to take a direct part (see Figure 5.10). One junior English class suggested that each person monitor their own behavior daily. They started with index cards that described how they had been behaving and what they planned to do. Then, every day, the cards were passed back during the last 5 minutes of class. Students wrote down the date and responded to this prompt: "What did you do today that contributed positively to class and helped you meet your goal?" After a couple of weeks, the class decided they didn't need the cards anymore because their distracting behaviors were no longer an issue: they were now more conscious of their behavior choices and also found that class was less stressful and fun when everyone was respectful and ready to positively engage in the day's learning.

Figure 5.10 **Juniors work collaboratively to brainstorm ideas and decide on some workable solutions to a problem.**

While the same "crowdsourcing" techniques can be used to solve problems related to learning, students are far less likely to share their academic struggles publicly. The important thing to remember is to ask students for suggestions in writing. Noticing that some of her students were having difficulty engaging in meaningful choice reading, Lindsey Jones posed this question: "What would help you enjoy reading more and become a better reader?" The response in Figure 5.11 echoed the thoughts of

Teachers have made reading not fun. They torture us by giving us worksheets with the book instead of letting us just read it. They give out essays to write. It just ruins a book. It gets rid of the whole purpose of a book which is to read for fun.

Figure 5.11 **While the previous example shows how students can set goals and monitor their own behavior in order to solve a problem, this eighth-grade student gave an honest response when Lindsey Jones elicited ideas from her students on how she could help them become stronger readers.**

quite a few students. Though Lindsey's class was not worksheet driven, several comments similar to this one made her keenly aware of how many students were among the "reading wounded." After years of worksheet-based instruction in previous grades, they had come to negatively associate reading with worksheets, which had soured them on reading. Knowing this enabled Lindsey to open up a discussion with her class about how people become better readers as well as assure her students that reading—at least in her classroom—would never become a march through a worksheet packet (see Figure 5.12).

Figure 5.12 **Solving the worksheet problem freed these eighth graders to start enjoying the opportunity to peruse new additions to the classroom library. Here, students are looking through stacks of new books and noting their opinions on "book scorecards," which they will refer to later when choosing new titles to read.**

Goal: Bolster Alliances

Lessons to support this goal:

- Observe a Success and Document It in a Positive Note (page 181)

- Turn Conference Night into a Conversation About Learning (page 186)

- Create Partnerships When Communicating with Parents and Guardians (Even During Tough Conversations) (page 189)

TRADITIONAL APPROACH	COLLABORATIVE APPROACH
• Misbehavior is more likely to be recognized and called out than successful behavior. • Parent/guardian–teacher conferences focus on grades. • Phone calls to parents or guardians focus on negative reporting and a request to the family member to "fix the problem."	• Teachers are avid "kid-watchers," keenly observing successes and readily sharing those observations with parents or guardians and students. • Conference night is presented as an opportunity to celebrate learning. • Phone calls to students' families are presented as an opportunity for collaborative problem-solving.
⬇ LEADS TO ⬇	⬇ LEADS TO ⬇
Ø The attention students get for misbehavior reinforces that behavior. Ø Depending on the student's current grade, conferences offer parents or guardians a chance to feel proud or demoralized, but no one really has the chance to examine actual learning. Ø Though a phone call to a parent or guardian may end with the family member promising to talk to their child, it also often ends with a tone of tension and discord.	✔ Students and parents or guardians feel affirmed and appreciated for the positive contributions made in class. ✔ Students and parents or guardians feel proud and empowered when celebrating learning accomplishments. ✔ Parents and guardians feel heard and feel connected to their student's classroom success, and therefore are more likely to work with teachers to support their child's success at school.

Figure 5.13

MOVE>Observe a Success and Document It in a Positive Note

Immediate Result: From day one, being on the lookout for shareable student successes reframes your orientation for what you notice and remember. Rather than zooming in on student misbehavior and deficiency (a natural tendency because *this* was the type of teaching so often modeled in our own years as students), we actively work to retrain ourselves to zoom in on what students are doing well, redefining deficiencies as areas for potential growth. Additionally, your students get a happy surprise when they hear that you've sent a positive note to their families.

Long-Term Result: Each positive note you send a family about a student affirms their successful guidance as well as the potential of a child they love—a great way to build a trusting relationship. Additionally, a positive note creates a bridge between family and teacher. That note fosters a first impression that you are paying attention to your students and know them as individuals. As a result, students are more likely to view you as an ally than as an adversary.

Stop for a second and think about the time it takes to hammer out a "bad news" email or make a "bad news" phone call. And then think about how effective those communications are overall. When we connect with families over a negative issue, there's almost always an underlying tension that remains in that relationship as this less-than-spectacular story becomes part of your shared history. Even if the issue is eventually resolved, no one in the story feels particularly satisfied. So, instead of initiating contact when a problem arises, how about initiating contact daily with some good news?

At the end of each day, set a goal for yourself to jot off positive messages to the parents or guardians of five of your students: emails, handwritten and mailed notes, text messages, or messages sent through your school's learning management system. While you might choose a phone message, a piece of writing is more tangible and harder to forget or overlook. It can be printed out and reread. Detail specific observations of positive ways each student participated and contributed to class. The notes don't have to be long: five or six sentences, maybe one hundred words. Eventually, every student's family will receive one, but start with the students who might need a little shot of positivity the most.

As you work to hit that five-note-a-day goal, it will make you a better kid-watcher. For some kids, you'll find it's super easy to collect positive anecdotes, but for others you'll sometimes come up empty. Don't give up or feel frustrated—just push yourself a little harder to pay attention to the kids who are quiet as well as the ones who get your attention because of their frequent need for redirection. And that's when you'll begin to see those students whom you might previously have labeled "disruptive" in a completely new light. Disruptive students aren't disruptive all the time. As a matter of fact, lots of times they are following directions and contributing positively to class. Unfortunately, because we teachers expect perfection 100 percent of the time, we get blinded by that narrowly focused lens. Once you readjust your point of view, you'll have lots of success stories to write home about for every student.

So what would these notes look like? Here are a couple of examples:

Hello Mrs. Galla,

I just wanted to drop a quick note to tell you about Henry's contribution in class today. As I was observing him in his table group discussing the causes of the Civil War, Henry noticed one member who was pretty quiet. First, he nudged his partner and quietly checked to see if she was feeling okay. Then, since she was, he reentered the discussion, but when there was a pause, he said, "We haven't heard what Susan thinks. Let's listen to her now." And Susan shared some great ideas, ideas that no one would have heard if it hadn't been for Henry!

Hello Mr. Smith,

As we are finishing up our unit on *Othello*, I just wanted to let you know what a fantastic job Ron did interpreting his lines and playing Iago. Not only were his lines perfectly memorized, but so was his blocking. Everyone in the room loved his performance, applauding wildly when the scene was concluded. Ron certainly showed everyone he has a hidden talent for acting. I am so happy that I was able to video record his performance because I know it will inspire future classes as they work on perfecting their own *Othello* scene performances.

When you take a look at both of these notes, notice the specific recipe pieces:

1. The note describes a specific anecdote, detailing exactly what the student said or did.

2. If possible, the note also includes how this student's actions affected another student or the class positively.

3. The note makes absolutely no mention of previous problems or deficiencies. Its entire purpose is to celebrate a classroom success that the student generated under their own power.

For almost every note, you'll find that families are effusively appreciative. These emails break the ice and create a strong bond. We teachers might not realize it, but middle school and high school can be confusing times for parents and guardians. When children are in elementary school, parents and guardians have to maintain contact with only one or two teachers. The departmentalization of middle school and high school can overwhelm parents and guardians: now a student might have six or seven different teachers. A positive email builds a bridge between you and a parent or guardian, and it demonstrates that their child isn't just one more student in your classroom; you know them as an individual. Also, if you print out a copy of the email, it's a nice way to build a bond with students as well. At the end of class, catch the student at the door, hand them the email printout, and say, "Hey, I thought you might enjoy reading this. It's great having you in class. Thanks!" (see Figure 5.14).

Figure 5.14 **When students know their teacher notices and acknowledges their successes, they enter the room in a positive, cooperative mind frame, ready to enjoy class.**

Now, you might still be thinking, "It might take me 5 minutes a note. Where am I going to find an extra 25 minutes per day outside class?" Try taking a close look at

- **Grading:** Are you seeing positive results from copious notes on drafts, or do you see more progress in a conference with a student during class time? Do *all* your quizzes need to be graded by you rather than by your students? Does *every* small assignment need a grade? Teach your students how to accurately self-evaluate and set goals for themselves (see Chapter 4, page 154), and you'll find that you have more time to focus on positive contact with families.

- **Negative contact with families:** If you are spending an inordinate amount of time getting in contact with families over negative issues, consider how productive that time has been. Has it resulted in positive change or in stress and antagonizing conversations? Switching gears to focus on positives when contacting families could go a long way toward making calls about negative issues unnecessary (see Figure 5.15).

Student Name	Date Contacted	Contact Method	Message Summary
Anders, Steve	8.31	email	Kudos—invited others into conversation, tries even if he's wrong
Anders, Steve	12.17	email	Great attitude during stressful end-of-semester time, good responsibility reading the morning announcements
Craigs, Carrie	8.27	email	Kudos—great responsibility and enthusiasm for the school year (making to-do list, crossing things off)
Craigs, Carrie	8.29	email	Advisory intro & kudos for a great start to the year, helping a classmate write with broken wrist
Craigs, Carrie	12.1	email	Great Q2 essay—well done weaving texts and opinions together
Craigs, Carrie	12.14	email	Responsible, good writer
David, Alehandro	8.27	email	Advisory intro & kudos for great start to the year
David, Alehandro	9.13	email	Great start to the year—showing responsibility, hard work completing HW, 100 on signpost quiz, organized, diligent
Edwards, Imani	8.31	email	Advisory intro & good start to the year
Edwards, Imani	12.1	email	Great Q2 essay—impressive playing with quoting authors and stretching writing
Edwards, Imani	12.14	email	Great writing, nice work with a classmate on grammar
Grens, Dorothy	11.29	email	Kudos—great job trying Shakespeare out loud and asking questions/participating
Grens, Dorothy	12.12	email	Good job improving behavior and good essay grade for Q2 essay (95)
Grens, Dorothy	12.14	email	Great student—active participant—good writer
Germanotta, Angie	8.27	email	Advisory intro & kudos for a great start to the year
Germanotta, Angie	8.31	email	Kudos—awesome summer reading assignment
Germanotta, Angie	9.12	email	Low PR1 grade (68) due to missing summer reading assignment
Germanotta, Angie	11.29	email	Kudos—great average (90) and wonderful attitude in class
Germanotta, Angie	12.7	email	Joy to have in class! So polite and so kind.
Germanotta, Angie	12.12	email	Great job reading Shakespeare aloud with energy and emotion!
Gonzalez, Larry	8.27	email	Welcome & kudos—eager to learn, great help to new students, good responsibility
Gonzalez, Larry	8.31	email	Kudos—great work on summer reading assignment
Gonzalez, Larry	9.12	email	Great to have in class! Interest in grammar, positive personality.
Gonzalez, Larry	11.1	email	Follow up to conversation with student (went well) & natural conversation later in class
Gonzalez, Larry	11.31	BB game	Great drive to do well! Nice recent homework.
Gonzalez, Larry	12.12	email	Great energy in class
Moore, Jasmine	8.27	email	Advisory intro & great start to the year
Moore, Jasmine	9.12	email	Low PR1 grade (65)
Moore, Jasmine	10.1	email	Good energy & focus after school holiday
Moore, Jasmine	10.12	email	Improvements with vocab work--on track to see higher grades
Moore, Jasmine	11.8	email	Low PR2 grade (67)
Moore, Jasmine	11.29	email	Good dedication to making S1 essay really good; nice focus
Moore, Jasmine	11.31	email	Great personality and upbeat spirit (esp. with grammar work)
Moore, Jasmine	12.13	email	Great attitude, responsibility—able to separate social and academic focus
Moore, Jasmine	12.14	email	Good work in class on final essay. Hoping she brings paragraphs at study hall to get feedback.

Figure 5.15 Seventh-grade teacher Lauren Huddleston always resolved to write positive emails, but noticed her follow-through fell by the wayside around October. Instead of losing momentum again, Lauren kept herself accountable by setting up a parent contact spreadsheet. Each entry included the date, contact method, and a summary of the message, green for positive and red for negative. Now Lauren was able to quickly review her contacts' home so that no one was left out.

MOVE> Turn Conference Night into a Conversation About Learning

> **Immediate Result:** Rather than reporting (or quibbling about) a student's grades, you and the student's parent or guardian are able to celebrate the student's accomplishments and set attainable learning goals.
>
> **Long-Term Result:** Students see themselves as having agency in their own learning. Parents and guardians may be more enthusiastic allies if they see how they can help by giving their children positive support in their learning endeavors rather than punishment for falling short.

A very disturbing report was released at the end of 2018, linking the arrival of report cards to spikes in physical abuse of children (Bright et al. 2018). While the study's aim was to explain that releasing report cards on Friday had the worst outcomes for children, the fact that there is *any* relation between report cards and abuse is sobering. It becomes incumbent on us to consider the effects grades have on our students. How can we help keep the focus on celebrating students' growth rather than on rewards or punishments? One way is to reframe the conversations that happen on conference night.

First, now that most districts have moved to online grading and families can see students' grades on individual assignments, it's time to stop placing a focus on the screen during conferences. Instead, focus on sharing concrete, tangible examples of student work. This work might be contained in physical folders, a student-kept three-ring notebook, or an online file the student keeps for each class. But here's the catch: instead of setting up these collections yourself, have your *students* prepare for conferences by creating a reflective portfolio. Block out about two class periods for this preparation.

During the first period, give students some sticky notes and encourage them to really look at their artifacts, marking the ones with sticky notes that best reflect their accomplishments and illustrate personal growth. Once these preliminary choices are made, have students sort their pieces into two different folders: one for accomplishments and one for growth. Finally have students return to the items in each folder and choose four pieces: the two artifacts that best represent academic accomplishment thus far and the two artifacts that demonstrate an opportunity for growth. If students have been sorting electronically, ask them to save their selections to a clearly marked folder that you have access to. Alternatively, you can ask them for printouts.

Next, on small, note-sized papers, or in a new document in their digital folders, ask students to write about why they chose the artifact and what it shows about their academic accomplishment or their opportunity for growth. If students are working with hard copies, have them attach each note to its artifact.

In the second class period, the fun begins! Students pair up with their folders. In turn, one student takes on the role of parent or guardian while the other student explains their artifacts. Those playing students are coached not to read from their notes, but to use the ideas they wrote down as a starting place for explaining the meaning behind the chosen artifacts. The "adult's" job is to seriously interview their "child" about the artifacts. Follow-up questions that elicit additional details are expected. After about 5 minutes, have student switch roles. Of course, while students are being interviewed by their "family member," you are listening in, learning about their artifact choices, and jotting down the questions from the "adult" partners that really get the students to explain their artifacts.

Finish up by citing the tremendous thinking and reflection that creating and talking about their work required. You might also create a class list of the best questions—questions that they'd like their own family members to ask them on conference night, or that they might bring up if their adults don't think of them. Collect the portfolios and encourage students to attend conferences with their family member so

Figure 5.16 Conference night offers this family an opportunity to talk about their daughter's thinking behind her Funds of Knowledge map (see page 129). Notice that when students are ready to talk about their work, the teacher need not guide the discussion!

that they can be the ones to talk about their work in the class (see Figure 5.16). However, if an adult turns up without their student in tow, you will still be able to show them the portfolio and talk from their notes as you look at and celebrate the work together. Ideally, this kind of conferencing creates energy and the commitment to continuing academic achievement that is often lacking when we all sit around the computer looking at columns of numbers.

MOVE>Create Partnerships When Communicating with Parents and Guardians (Even During Tough Conversations)

Immediate Result: Having a plan for parent or guardian communications means you are always ready to address concerns from within the classroom or from the parent or guardian.

Long-Term Result: Opening an understanding and empathetic avenue of dialogue creates a much greater likelihood that parents and guardians will become your allies, collaborating with you so that their child is successful.

Probably one of the hardest roles of a teacher is to call a student's family about a concern. Another equally difficult role is returning a phone call from a parent or guardian who is clearly angry. In either case, it's important to remember that these adults are sending the best children they've got to school—the children they've raised and loved. This is an area where we proceed with care: poorly considered actions or word choices can alienate both child and their family member.

Before You Call

1. **Determine if a phone call is required.**
   If you have already worked with the student on this issue but the problem is not turning around, it's time to call the parents or guardians. Most parents or guardians would rather know about an issue earlier than later, when a problem appears insurmountable.

2. **Gather necessary documentation.**
   If you are calling about an academic issue, make sure you have the student's work in hand.

If you are calling about a behavior issue, write down the actions of concern in objective language. What did the student say? What actions did they take? What effect did the actions have on their learning as well as the learning environment for other students? Avoid words that label, such as *rude*, *defiant*, *silly*, or *apathetic*.

3. **Determine the desired resolution.**

   Know why you're calling before you call. Do you just want the parent or guardian to be aware of the situation? Is there something that the parent or guardian might do at home that could help resolve the problem?

4. **List the positives.**

   Take a minute to think about what positive behaviors—academic or social— you've seen from this student. Not only will having these in mind help the person you're about to call understand that you care about their child; it will also help you consider the whole student—not just the part that's currently having an issue.

5. **Put yourself in the parent's or guardian's position.**

   When you call to discuss any student problem, it is a disappointment for the parent or guardian. Humans are highly sensitive to criticism. They may not even hear the problem because all they will hear in their head is "I'm a bad parent" or "I'm not doing right by this kid." If they become defensive, continue to remain calm and reassuring. Take some deep breaths, let them talk, and commit to listening. As long as they are not abusive, do give them the opportunity to speak. Quite often, it is this non-interrupting, devoted listening that makes a parent or guardian feel respected and heard. And once parents and guardians feel you are on their side, a resolution that all parties can live with is far more likely.

Making the Call

1. **Identify yourself.**

   Say hello and identify yourself by your first and last name. Continue by stating the student, the class, and the school name.

   Hi, this is Nancy Steineke. I'm Jon's English teacher at Andrew High School.

2. Request permission.

Before jumping into the reason for your call, make sure the parent or guardian has the time to talk. And then pause to let them absorb the fact that you are calling. Remember, teachers don't generally call with good news.

> *I'd like to talk to you about Jon's work in class. Do you have a couple of minutes?*

3. Begin with the positives.

Name some specific instances of praiseworthy behavior you've noticed.

> *Jon really brings something to the classroom. All of the students appreciate his friendliness and willingness to include everyone. Last week, when a transfer student joined the class, Jon unhesitantly volunteered to work with the new student.*

4. Listen for a response.

Now that the person on the other end of the line has had a moment to get over the initial shock of hearing from you and to collect themselves, pause a moment to listen. They might bring up the problem you were just going to mention, or they might even bring up an issue that you were completely unaware of: an impending divorce, a family illness, the death of a close relative. If they share a recent traumatic situation, let them know that the school is available to help. For example:

> *I am so sorry for your loss. I was completely unaware of this; thank you for telling me about this situation. Do you think it would be helpful for Jon to talk with our social worker about it? Our social worker is very discreet. After an initial meeting, Jon could decide whether or not to continue the meetings. Would you like me to contact our social worker so that she can arrange to talk with Jon?*

Most of the time parents and guardians are very open when this option is offered to a student who is struggling with issues beyond the classroom. Also, most parents and guardians are reluctant to directly contact the school social worker themselves and are relieved that you will take on this responsibility.

5. **Present the issue in objective language.**

   Focus solely on describing the student's behavior. Avoid "*I* messages" in this description—they shift the attention back to you.

   > *Jon has trouble confining his talking to appropriate times. He often talks when it is time to work silently and independently. When I redirect him to the work at hand, he works for 2 or 3 minutes but then strikes up another conversation. I've talked with Jon a few times about his inappropriately timed talking. Jon is always apologetic, but his behavior doesn't change.*

6. **Pose a question that defers expertise to the parent or guardian.**

   If the parent or guardian has a helpful suggestion, that's wonderful. If not, asking is still a helpful way to communicate that you respect and value their role and their insights.

   > *What are some ideas you might have that would help me support Jon in curbing his off-task talking? What might work best for him?*

7. **Pause, listen, and take notes.**

   Pay close attention to any concerns the parent or guardian shares. Again, if it turns out there are difficult circumstances that the student is facing, ask if it would be all right to share them with the guidance counselor or social worker. Also, be alert to a parent or guardian who might be inclined to react in a disparaging way toward their child, either with language or threat of physical punishment. Remind the parent or guardian of their child's strengths and accomplishments. Directly state that corporal punishment is ineffective when it comes to changing behavior positively. If the parent or guardian does not calm down, it is advisable to confer with an administrator. Do not keep the knowledge of a possibly abusive person to yourself.

8. **End by thanking them for collaborating with you, by focusing on a positive outcome for the student, and by arranging a follow-up call.**

   Making a plan to keep in touch communicates that this is a priority for you.

   > *Thank you so much for collaborating with me just now. I know that we all really want Jon to succeed and realize his potential. I appreciate the time you*

took and the insight and ideas you shared with me just now. Would it be all
right if we touched base again in a week so that I can update you on how
things are going?

Steps for Returning a Parent's or Guardian's Angry Phone Message or Email

Sooner or later, every teacher will receive an angry phone message or email from a parent or guardian. Because we are human, our first reaction is to become defensive and, possibly, angry ourselves. Before engaging in any communication, the first step is to calm ourselves down, take some deep breaths, and remember that though the parent or guardian might have been aggressive and demanding, the message stemmed from their desire to protect their child. So, what can you do to enlist this parent or guardian as an ally rather than an adversary?

1. **Solve the problem with a phone call.**

   It is easy for an email conflict to escalate: words without any other context create the opportunity for misreading and misinterpretation. So, whether the conversation began as an angry email or an angry phone call, continue the conversation via phone. A phone conversation offers give-and-take, the opportunity to ask follow-up questions and request clarification in real time. Also, a phone call enables you to hear the person's tone of voice, a piece of very important information when you are working together to solve a problem. In contrast, emails offer no vocal clues or conversation, only responses back and forth.

2. **Acknowledge you've received the message.**

   As soon as possible, send an email stating that you have received the message and look forward to talking with them soon in a phone call. An initial email response is better than a phone call: it's important to connect immediately so that the parent or guardian does not feel ignored or insulted, but responding with a phone call immediately won't give you time to prepare before the conversation. Then give them a choice of times when you can call them. While it might be more convenient for parents or guardians to talk in the evening, for personal teacher health, I strongly recommend confining stressful situations to work hours and to your official school phone number.

If you feel it is necessary, you can also leave a phone message. Call just before you have to head for class to acknowledge you received the message, not to solve the problem.

> *Hi, Mrs. Smith. Thank you for calling this morning and sharing your concerns with me. I look forward to talking with you. I can give you a call tomorrow at 7:30 a.m. before first hour or at 11:45 a.m. during my preparation period. Which would you prefer?*

3. **Prepare for the call.**

   If you received an email, print it out and identify specific concerns and questions that the parent or guardian would like addressed. If you received a phone call, listen to the recording and take notes. Then gather any pertinent data you'll need in your discussion. Also, jot down some positive comments about the student that you can share with the parent or guardian.

4. **Make the call.**

   Take some deep breaths and calm yourself. Before you dial, remember that every parent or guardian has their child's best interest at heart. Dial, greet them, and ask them to tell you about their concerns. Listen. Take notes. Ask clarification questions. Do not react to insults or accusations. Do not become defensive. Keep listening. Often the problem-solving process requires you to allow parents or guardians to vent; many times you can de-escalate the conflict just by giving them the chance to be heard and responding calmly and empathetically. This is why I don't recommend that you return the phone call immediately: You need the time and calm mind frame to prepare yourself to manage this call. Continue to remind yourself not to take it personally and not to get defensive. Parents' or guardians' frustrations emerge for many different reasons, most of them sprouting from a trigger other than the teacher, yet the teacher is often the recipient of the venting of these frustrations. The best way to work with the parent or guardian is to imagine how you would want to be treated if the roles were reversed.

> *Hi, Mrs. Smith. I'm returning your call from yesterday. Is this still a good time to talk? Please tell me about your concerns regarding _____ . . . . I understand you're upset. . . . I'm not sure what you mean by _____ . Can you give me an example? . . . I want to make sure I'm hearing you correctly; tell me if I'm accurately summarizing what you've said.*

5. **If necessary, investigate further.**

   Though teachers are supposed to have eyes in the back of their heads, we still don't see or witness everything that occurs in our classroom. Sometimes parents or guardians call to report altercations between students of which, until that moment, you were unaware. Or a parent or guardian might ask you a question for which you don't have an accurate answer. In either case, reassure them that you will look into the matter and get back to them. Propose a reasonable timeline for gathering the missing information, and establish a time for a follow-up phone appointment.

6. **Work toward a resolution.**

   Once you have heard the parent or guardian completely, thank them for being so willing to share with you. If you made a mistake or an unintentional misstep, apologize. Remind them again that you are members of the same team: both of you want to see the child do their very best in class, and you really want to work with them so that this can be achieved. Then ask them how they would like to see their concern addressed. If they make a suggestion that is reasonable and in the best interest of their child, agree to follow through. If you truly believe you cannot follow through on the initial suggestion, offer some possible choices and explain how they might influence the student positively.

   > *Thank you so much for sharing your concerns with me. I'm sorry you had to come to me with this, but I know this conversation is going to help us work together since we both want the same thing: we want to see Jon succeed in school and this class. What can we do together to solve this problem?*

In many cases, the parent or guardian will now be calm enough to offer a reasonable solution, but if it is something you are unable to execute, be honest and offer some alternative choices.

I'm sorry, Mrs. Smith, I don't think I'd be able to follow through on that suggestion, but I do have some other ideas that might work. Would you like to hear them?

7. **Conclude the conversation.**
   Repeat the solution that you've both agreed upon, thank the parent or guardian for bringing the problem to your attention, and let them know that you will give them a call in a few days to tell them how things are going.

8. **Complete your notes and contact your immediate supervisor.**
   Jot down everything you can about the phone call: specifics discussed, the solution agreed upon, the date of the call, and the time it began and ended. Then arrange to talk to your immediate supervisor. While you may have solved this problem to the parent's or guardian's satisfaction, it is helpful for your immediate supervisor to know the details of the conversation as well as what steps you agreed to take to ameliorate the problem. That way, if the parent or guardian does contact your supervisor, that supervisor will know the background and be able to support you.

9. **Follow up.**
   Call the parent or guardian as promised, let them know how the solution is working, report as many positives about their child as you possibly can, and assure them that you want an open line of communication.

Hi, Mrs. Smith, I just wanted to get back to you and let you know that the plan we worked out for Jon is successful. He's been much more focused on his classwork, and other students look forward to working with him because he is so dependable. Thank you so much for working together with me to meet our goal of helping Jon be more successful in class. If you ever have any other concerns, please do not hesitate to contact me.

If, at any point, a parent or guardian becomes abusive in their language or threatening, stay calm but inform the parent or guardian that the call cannot continue.

> *I know how concerned you are about Jon, but both of us need to be in a calm, problem-solving state of mind so that we can work together on this issue. I will contact you again in a few days. Thank you for your concern.*

After you terminate the call, add as many specific details to your notes as you can, including direct quotes. Then meet with your immediate supervisor as soon as possible so that together you can discuss the correct course of action. When you meet with your supervisor, encourage them to contact your building principal as well, as the parent or guardian may quickly decide to contact those they consider "above" you. Also, talk with the student's guidance counselor. If they have dealt with this family before, they may be able to give you some insight and tips on how to handle future encounters. Finally, if you feel intimidated by this parent or guardian, insist that you have an administrator present for any future contacts, whether it be a conference call or a face to face meeting.

Goal: Get Back on Track

Lessons to support this goal:

- Address Issues Without Escalating the Situation (page 199)

- Invite Students to Document Their Behavior (page 206)

- Confer with Students to Help Them Recognize and Revise Ineffective Behavior (page 208)

- Keep a Record of Your Problem-Solving (page 213)

- Use a Proactive Approach with Supervisors, Deans, Principals, and Guidance Counselors (page 216)

TRADITIONAL APPROACH	COLLABORATIVE APPROACH
• The teacher takes student misbehavior personally and consequently makes emotional, impulsive decisions. • The teacher tells students what behavior is expected but does not help them develop the self-regulation to achieve the desired behavior. • When the teacher's attempts to solve behavior problems fail, the problems are referred to administrators for fixing.	• The teacher consciously focuses on maintaining a positive mindset while avoiding emotional traps that lead to bad decisions. • The teacher actively works with students to understand problems and then confers with students to solve the problems. • The teacher considers community-building efforts with each and every student and their parents or guardians.
⬇ LEADS TO ⬇	⬇ LEADS TO ⬇
∅ Emotionally generated teacher decisions seldom solve the problem, model irrational behavior, and lead to deteriorating teacher–student relationships. ∅ While a short-term student behavior change may occur, a permanent behavior change is unlikely. ∅ Though an administrator has the power to enforce a punishing consequence, the teacher–student relationship may be damaged and permanent behavior change is unlikely when that student returns to the classroom.	✔ Students recognize that the teacher is trying hard to see them at their best because the teacher calmly responds to classroom behavior management issues. ✔ Students are empowered, learning to reflect upon, discuss, and change unhelpful behaviors. ✔ Administrators take on the role of collaborators who are invested in student success rather than disciplinarians who mete out punishment.

Figure 5.17

MOVE> Address Issues Without Escalating the Situation

Immediate Result: When faced with an unforeseen issue, you can handle it effectively in the moment without it spiraling out of control.

Long-Term Result: Addressing disruptions respectfully, calmly, and effectively demonstrates to students that they can trust you to keep their learning space safe. As a result, they can focus on their learning when they're in your class. As you make a habit of addressing issues without escalating them, you'll have an increased sense of confidence and agency and higher morale in general, which are linked to both high student achievement and a greater chance that you will choose to stay in the field (Leithwood and McAdie 2007).

Much of the work outlined in this book is about laying a foundation of trust and creating a classroom community, both of which will help prevent classroom disruptions. Yet, in even the most harmonious classroom community, disruptions will sometimes arise.

While there is no way to anticipate or design a plan for every possible issue, you can be prepared to make a game-time decision by knowing your options ahead of time. The following list is a distillation of what I have seen work in classrooms—my own and others'—for decades. As you read the suggestions below, consider how you could put each into action. Try to connect these suggestions to previous issues you've had to handle. What new options does this list provide when something similar happens in the future?

- **Remember that you can control only your own behavior.** Therefore, model the behavior you'd like your students to exhibit. This means remaining calm in both demeanor and voice. (Use polite language. Keep your phone in your pocket.) It also means not reacting immediately to the negative behavior of others. We tell students to walk away from a confrontation rather than staying to light the fuse. Teachers need to do the same.

- **Put yourself in the place of the student.** Think about what you're about to say: How would you feel if someone said that to you? Would it change your behavior or make you angry, sad, frustrated, misunderstood, or resentful? If your words might stir up negative emotions, the problem will not be solved and you are jeopardizing your relationship with that student as well.

- **Address off-task behavior with nonverbal cues.** If you're dealing with a minor disruption, simply letting the student know that you're aware of it may be enough to cue them to get back on track. Move into the student's area of proximity. Make eye contact with the student along with a slight shake of your head. Move away. Or move into proximity and silently tap the student's desk. Move away.

- **Always work from the mindset that students will cooperate.** Whenever possible, give students the option to decide to cooperate rather than ordering them to do something. For example, if a student frequently engages in off-task conversations, you might want to move them to a different seat. Rather than standing at the front of the room and telling the student to move their seat, you could lean in while the class is engaged in independent work and whisper to them, "Would you mind taking the seat over there?" If a student is slow to get started on the work, say, "I need you to get started now. How much do you think you can do in 10 minutes?" Or, if you can hook the student with a personal strength or expertise, use that. "You're interpretation of the reading always fascinates me; I'm looking forward to seeing what you conclude." Here's another: "This is the first time I've tried this assignment. After you're done, I want to hear what you thought was easy, hard, or confusing. Will you do that for me?" (Benson 2014, 148–49). After offering one of these invitations, wait for the student to respond, offer congratulations on their plan, and then move away. If they do not take you up on your invitation, don't badger, beg, or nag. Instead, catch up with that student at the end of class to discuss how to solve the problem at hand.

- **Use "*I* statements."** If you notice a behavior is distracting you in your teaching—and most likely distracting other students as well—take a moment when the class is working to privately whisper to the student, "When you shout across the room while I'm teaching, it makes it difficult for me to concentrate. When I can't do my best job, I feel sad and frustrated." More than likely, the student will offer a whispered apology once they understand how their behavior is affecting others. Remember, teen brains are wired for impulsitivy, so while shouting across the room is an obvious disruption to you, it really may not have been intended that way from the student's perspective. And even if a student offers an unempathetic response such as "So what!" calmly respond in a whisper, "I just wanted you to know how I felt, and I hope you will give it some thought. Thank you." And, as always, move on (Fay and Funk 1995, 337). Chances are that the unempathetic response was motivated by an attempt to save face in front of peers, something that is *very* important to teens. Moving on de-escalates potential conflict while still leaving the student with the knowledge that one's behaviors affect others.

- **Acknowledge emotions.** If you notice a student who is clearly upset (angry, sad, distracted, sullen), quietly say something like this: "You seem angry. Do you think you can concentrate on the classwork, or do you need to go someplace else to clear your head?" Most of the time, just acknowledging a student's feelings begins to calm them down and enable them to continue with the classwork. However, if a student does need an escape, be sure to have your options worked out ahead of time. "What place would work best for you? I know I could give you a pass to the guidance office, the nurse, or Mr. Howard's class since he has some empty seats in the back of the room. I'm going to miss you and you're going to miss today's work, so if you start to feel better and are up to returning, just ask for a pass back to class." Of course, follow up with that student as soon as possible and listen to what they have to say. Then ask them what they need from you.

- **Enlist students to help you do a better job.** When a student's behavior is distracting you (talking, fidgeting, pen tapping, texting) say, "It's hard for me to concentrate and be a good teacher when your _____ is distracting me. Would you be willing to help me do my best job? [It's hard for a student to answer no to that.] Okay, at the end of class let's take for a couple of minutes to work this out. I need your advice." And then work out a solution together. It might be that the student just needs a private silent signal from you as a reminder to curb the behavior. It might be that the student needs a way to fidget or pen tap that isn't so distracting. It might be a change *you* need to make! The only way you can remedy the situation is to collaboratively and calmly solve the problem.

- **Whenever possible, offer choices.** When students—or adults—have the opportunity to solve a problem via an outcome they choose, it enables them to feel in control of the situation because they are the decision makers. However, for this strategy to work, the choices have to be equally attractive and positive. Here's an example of a choice that does not meet those criteria: "You can complete the assignment now or receive a zero. Which would you prefer?" On the other hand, if the student is not disturbing others with their noncompliance, here's a pair of choices that does meet the criteria: "You can complete the assignment now or do it for homework. Which do you prefer?" And if the answer is "homework," ask this follow-up question: "What's your plan to make sure you'll get it done later?" That second question might be all that is needed for the student to reconsider and use the time at hand (Fay and Funk 1995, 144).

- **When a student rejects you, do not give up.** Continue to treat the student with friendliness, respect, and appreciation. Keep noticing strengths and accomplishments—big or small—and share them with the student. Rejection is a means of protection and also control. When students make themselves unlikable, they can accurately predict that their teachers will ignore them and won't like them. Find the strength to break the cycle of their self-fulfilling prophecy (Benson 2014).

- **Think about what the student wants or needs.** Challenging students behave in disruptive ways in order to fulfill needs. Students may act out because of academic frustration. They may be reacting to circumstances of which we are unaware. Our job is to continue to offer these students positive support and develop the trusting relationships necessary for them to let us know what they need.

- **Engage students in solving their own problems.** First, help students think out loud about what triggers unhelpful behaviors. Then ask them what they might do instead that will meet their needs using positive behavior choices. If a student responds with the classic "I don't know," offer wait time rather than immediately jumping in with your own advice. And after some wait time, if the student still has not come up with some solutions, ask, "I've thought of a couple of ideas—would you like to hear them?" And then offer those ideas as possibilities to consider rather than ultimatums. It's likely that once the student hears a couple of your ideas, they will think of something that will work even better for them. Plus, solving your own problems is empowering.

- **Channel patience.** When a student exhibits chronic misbehavior, it is something the student has been practicing long before they met you. While you work with that student to help them make better behavior choices, don't expect things to consistently go smoothly: changing one's comfortable, familiar behavior patterns is hard and uncomfortable. After all, if changing behavior were easy, there wouldn't be so many diet programs on the market! Students will have false starts, setbacks, and plateaus. Embrace the opportunity to persuade your students that different behaviors will benefit them and result in feeling better about themselves as well.

- **Pretend you are a proud grandparent.** When you find a student difficult to work with, imagine this scenario: You are that student's grandparent. You have run across a friend at the grocery store and you start bragging about your grandchild. Now, grab a piece of paper and write down all those brags—their strengths, their interests, their style, and any opportunities they have. Keep the focus on what this student *can* do. If you have lots to write down, you have multiple ways to start connecting with that student in positive ways. Capitalize on what this student has expertise in and ask them to advise *you*! Also, if your list is on the short side, this indicates that you need to get to know that student better so that you can notice and call out that student's strengths (Benson 2014).

- **Remember that everyone wants to save face.** Trying to save face is the crux of all power struggles. If you do offer an intervention whisper, don't be surprised if you hear an "under the breath" comment as you walk away. Instead of turning around and uttering the classic "What did you just say?"—keep walking. If the student *didn't* murmur something, they'd lose face with their classmates. Plus, we teachers always tell students to walk away from a provocation rather than getting into a fight. This is the perfect moment for you to model calmly walking away rather than "biting the hook" (Mendler, Curwin, and Mendler 2008, 33, 105).

- **Steer clear of rewards and punishments.** Depending on our own experiences, classroom management might have encompassed both. The most common example nowadays is the behavior chart. Everyone's clip starts on green and then travels up to sunshine and rainbows or down into thunderstorm territory depending on how compliant each student is throughout the day. While enough rainbows might result in a tangible reward, repeated thunderstorms earn a negative consequence, which is really just a different word for punishment. Plus, demoting a student to "thunderstorms" amounts to public humiliation, a form of bullying. Whether a student is defined by rainbows or thunderstorms, neither student is internalizing anything useful about choosing positive, beneficial behaviors. Instead, students are learning to behave in a coercive environment. Though compliance might be achieved in the moment, neither bribes nor punishments will help student make better behavior choices or extinguish negative, unhelpful, harmful behaviors. Finally, punishment often results in anger and weakens the relationship between the teacher and the student. Punishment is adversarial and results in "us versus them" thinking.

- **Address issues with individuals, not with the class as a whole.** As mentioned in the previous bullet point, punishment is largely ineffective in persuading students to change their behavior choices. Whenever an entire class is punished, the negative ramifications are amplified. Being punished for other classmates' misbehavior frustrates, angers, and disappoints students—especially students whose behavior was just fine. In their eyes, the teacher is patently unfair and cannot be trusted. Also, it is more than likely that the innocent students do not have the power and status necessary to use their peer pressure to persuade the real perpetrators to change their ways. However, a class punishment does have one strong unifying effect: it quickly unites the entire class against the teacher!

- **Refuse to argue.** Sometimes when you attempt to redirect a student, you'll be met with an argument. Don't take the bait. Instead, you can say, "It sounds like you want to argue, and you may be right. Let me think about this and get back to you. Since I've got to get back to teaching, we can't talk right now. When do you want to get together? We can talk before school, after school, or during genius hour. When do you want to schedule our talk?" Arguing is a practiced, knee-jerk response for some students, so sometimes the response will be "Forget about it; I'm okay" because the student just wasn't that invested in the argument to begin with. And if the student does want to schedule a time for "argument," great. But when you meet, let the student argue while you listen and then ask some follow-up questions so that you understand what might be behind that student's behavior. Then try to address *that* concern with the student.

- **De-escalate a power struggle by changing course with an off-topic question.** "Hey, those are really cool shoes. Are they comfy, too?" "I've been meaning to ask you: I know you know a lot about music—do you have any recommendations for my in-class Spotify playlist?" Of course, this only works if you stay calm and if you are genuinely interested in the answer (Plevin 2016, 243). The hope is that your question will be so unexpected that it defuses some anger and might even move the student to a frozen moment of stillness followed by a chuckle. Now you have the opportunity to ask the student if the problem-solving can be scheduled for after you finish up teaching.

- **Reframe a student's negative behavior in a positive light.** When a student is pushing your buttons, take a step back and think. While the behavior does have negative impacts, it's also very successful. Stop to admire that and then figure out how you can use it when you discuss the behavior with the student. Instead of saying, "I'm sick and tired of your smart aleck comments," say, "You have the quickest wit of anyone I've ever known, but it makes me feel bad to be the butt of your jokes. Was hurting my feelings your intention?" More than likely, the student will say, "No, I just blurt out whatever I think of." Continue, "I didn't think so. How do you think you could share your comments with the class in ways that wouldn't be hurtful?" Now the conversation is started (Curwin, Mendler, and Mendler 2018).

- **Avoid taking student behavior personally.** This suggestion falls into the "easier said than done" category, but it truly is effective. As mentioned earlier, students fall into negative behavior patterns to deal with a need, more than likely a need that arose long before they entered your classroom. And as you keep replaying the incident in your head (something most of us have difficulty avoiding), use the technique of reframing (above) to turn lemons into lemonade!

MOVE> Invite Students to Document Their Behavior

Immediate Result: Asking students to write about an issue in the classroom puts an immediate stop to the interruption and requires students to focus on their own actions.

Long-Term Result: Writing about one's own behavior offers students insight into how one operates. As time goes on, this recognition enables students to make better choices, choices that enhance their own learning environment as well as that of those around them. Students recognize what triggers behaviors that aren't helpful in class and can be proactive in changing these behaviors. Additionally, you are better able to see reasons and patterns in student behavior.

Though it's often been claimed that teachers have eyes in the back of their heads, we don't. We see quite a bit because of our vigilance, but we don't see everything. Plus, even if we do see some problematic behavior, we often miss the inciting incident. As teachers, we've all heard "They started it!" more than once, and lots of times our response goes something like this: "Yes, but *you're* the one I saw in action."

After a frustrating exchange like this, eighth-grade English teacher Monifa Johnson decided on a new policy. Here's how she introduced it to her students:

> *If something is going on in the classroom that distracts me and keeps me from doing my best thinking, I know it is distracting others in the room as well. When this happens, here's the way I'll respond. First, I'll walk over to you and make some direct eye contact with you as a warning. But if that doesn't work, I'll be back to hand you a piece of paper and tell you to document your behavior. You'll put down the date and answer this question: "How does your behavior just now compare with our classroom expectations?" Then you'll explain in as much detail as possible what your part was in the distraction. Once you're finished, you're free to jump back into the class and offer some positive contributions. Later in the*

period, I'll pick up your documentation, and then toward the end of the period, I will meet with you and we can talk about what happened. Does anybody have any questions?

Monifa found that having students write about *only* their own behaviors shifted each student's attention from what someone else did to what *they* did, making their writing more about reflection than about blame. She advises to never get into a back-and-forth with a student. If a student refuses to document their behavior, she responds, "If you are having trouble putting your actions into words, it might be easier to write down the questions you have so that we have something to talk about later. Also, since a couple of other students have already started documenting their part in this incident, it would be a shame not to hear your side of the story." Generally, that last comment is enough to get 99 percent of the students who need to document their behavior started (see Figure 5.18). And after that final statement, Monifa gets right back to her teaching.

Monifa finds that, generally, after students document their behavior once or twice, cooperative and respectful behavior emerges and influences others positively. She also keeps the student documentation filed away just in case she needs to have a later conversation with a parent or guardian.

Christopher A.R.G.   **Today is April 14**

Here is what happened, but to understand it we must go back to the 7th grade. Back to my golden years where money grew on trees and people were always nice. Anyhow, there I was sitting on my desk learning like nobody has ever learned before. And listening, listening like no mortal has ever listened before. When all of the sudden I hear the words "We have a new student." The new student went by the name Amyria. Anyhow months went by and I didn't think much of her, but not until now, because she has called me out. And accused me of such atrocities. I am disgusted at the things she has said. However I must confess the truth, no matter how painful. Very well, the truth is . . . that I framed her.

Figure 5.18 **When students tell the story from their perspective while focusing on the facts of the incident, it becomes harder to blame others. Indeed, in the last line of this eighth grader's documentation, he admits that Amyria's version of the facts is indeed correct.**

MOVE>Confer with Students to Help Them Recognize and Revise Ineffective Behavior

Immediate Result: You move your problem-solving time to outside class time— preserving more instructional time and alleviating the pressure of trying to problem-solve in front of an audience.

Long-Term Result: One-to-one conferences can be useful in building bridges between you and your students. Conferencing to develop better behavior teaches students how to evaluate and turn nonproductive behavior habits around. Additionally, if further behavior issues arise, it will be easier to work with students with whom you've already conferenced with.

Sometimes, despite the T-charts discussed earlier in this chapter (see pages 171–174), despite the regular behavior self-evaluation tools introduced in Chapter 4 (see pages 154–155), a student will need more intensive help in turning unproductive behavior (social or academic) into behavior that is personally rewarding and also contributes positively to the classroom learning environment. While it is always important that you work with the student calmly and nonaggressively, it's even more important in these kinds of conferences. Your goal isn't to force the student to comply; it's to generate a positive outcome for all involved. Since this kind of conference requires privacy as well as a little extra time, it's best to work with the student to make an appointment for this conversation. Depending on how your school operates, this conference time might be before or after school, or during a student's study hall, advisory, or homeroom time. As a last resort, arrange for the guidance department to call the student down on a guidance pass and meet the student there to talk.

Structure these conferences using a note-taking form (see Figure 5.19 and Online Reference 5.2) that is based on the WDEP structure from the reality therapy

Name _____   **Date** _____

Conference Notes

Wants • What do you want?	
Doing • What are you doing in class now?	
Evaluation • How's what you're doing working out? Is it getting you what you want?	
Plan • What can you do instead that will get you what you want? • What help do you need from me? • When should we have an update conference to see how the plan is working?	

Figure 5.19 **This form is useful for helping a student think about their behavior as well as keeping a conference focused on calm, useful problem-solving.**

work of Dr. William Glasser (1988). Glasser developed a frame for examining behavior in four steps that is often referred to as WDEP:

W: Consider what the person **wants**.

D: Consider what the person is **doing**.

E: **Evaluate** whether what the person is doing is helping them get what they want.

P: **Plan** what can be done to get the person what they want.

Before the conference begins, review the student's interest inventory and pick out a couple of items you could use as icebreaking openers. When the student arrives, welcome them, thank them for coming in to talk, and devote a few minutes to small talk.

Remember, the student knows they're in trouble. Working to open the conference in a congenial way can reduce both your stress and theirs, enabling the two of you to better think and work together.

> *Jon, thanks for making the time to come and talk to me. I know you're busy. Before you came in, I was just looking over your interest inventory and noticed that you mentioned getting a puppy just before school started. How's he doing? He must be getting pretty big.*

Listen and ask follow-up questions. Proceed to the crux of the meeting only when you and the student appear relaxed.

> *Let's talk about how you're doing in class. While you talk, I'm going to take a few notes so that we can review what we've talked about. Jon, when you think about class, what would you like to get out of it? What do you want?*

Listen. If the student shares something that is important to them, honor that. Of course, it's not unusual for students to reply, "Nothing." Don't take this personally— they may never have thought about having goals for their classes, or they may not feel comfortable enough to talk openly about what they want. If the student doesn't give you a clear idea of their goal for the class, offer a baseline goal that they don't have to show any personal vulnerabilities to admit to. For example:

> *Okay, I know that Algebra 1 is a requirement for graduation, not something you had a choice about. Even so, I bet you'd like to pass so that you end the year with all your credits and don't have to go to summer school. Other things you want out of this class may come to mind, too, and if they do, I'm happy to talk about them with you. But, for now, just to help us move forward, we can work with the goal of passing the class.*

Next, ask the student to describe what they are currently doing in your class.

> *Jon, describe how you've been working and behaving in class lately.*

Listen and take notes. People often recognize their participation in unhelpful behaviors, but they're stuck in a rut. Habits are hard to break. If you're thinking about adding your own observations about the student's behavior at this point, first ask yourself: Are your observations so different from what the student is self-reporting that they're essential to mention? This process is about building students' sense of agency. Including unnecessary criticism isn't productive.

> *Jon, how does what you're currently doing help you or hurt you in terms of getting what you want—passing this class?*

Listen, take notes, and then continue.

> *To get the grade you want, what do you think you need to start doing instead? What's the plan?*

Listen and take notes (see Figure 5.20). Sometimes students will come up blank. Rather than lecturing or badgering, say, "I have a few ideas that might work for you. Would you like to hear them?" This gives the student the choice. They can say yes or they can start ticking off some of their own ideas. Affirm what the student suggests. Continue by asking how you can help the student achieve their goal.

> *This plan looks pretty solid. Is there any specific help you need from me so that you can do this?*

Then finish up.

> *I'm going to make a photocopy of this and then give the original to you. Before I do, take a look and see if I wrote down everything accurately and if I missed anything.*

Let the student take a look and then get the plan back. Finally, talk to the student about follow-up.

> *Any plan always needs to be reviewed from time to time in order to make sure it's working. Also, sometimes the initial ideas we have for a plan need to be revised. When do you want to touch base on how your plan is working?*

Set the time and date, write it down, look up, smile at the student, and shake their hand while saying, "That's a deal! Great working with you! See you in algebra!"

Remember to keep the plan review date. Having a plan as well as someone to help them implement it enables students to improve their behavior. When reviewing the plan with a student during the follow-up conference, begin by listing all the positives you've noticed since the last meeting. Then ask, "How is this plan working for you? What changes have you noticed in the way you are operating in class?" and let the

Name _____   Date _____

Conference Notes

Wants • What do you want?	*Pass Algebra —* *Would like at least* *a C*
Doing • What are you doing in class now?	*— Not bringing* *supplies/work to* *class* *— Talking when I* *should be working*
Evaluation • How's what you're doing working out? Is it getting you what you want?	*— Failing* *— Falling behind —* *don't understand* *stuff*
Plan • What can you do instead that will get you what you want? • What help do you need from me? • When should we have an update conference to see how the plan is working?	*— Do my work in* *class* *— Stop talking* *— Listen to you* *— Move seat nearer to* *front* *— Get into math* *tutoring homeroom* *— Next Tuesday at* *end of class before* *lunch*

Figure 5.20 Example conference notes

student do most of the talking. Wrap up the conversation by summarizing what you've heard the student say, and ask the student what help they need from you, if any. Be sure to decide when the next update meeting should take place. Of course, if the student isn't following through on the initial plan, you can move the review date up to discuss what isn't working and why, so you can revise the existing plan.

MOVE>Keep a Record of Your Problem-Solving

Immediate Result: Keeping a written record of your problem-solving can help you ensure that you've dealt with the problem thoroughly in the moment.

Long-Term Result: As you build your written record, you'll have data that will help you see patterns in your students and in yourself. Additionally, if you must write a discipline referral or call a parent or guardian, you'll be able to easily outline the previous attempts you've made as a teacher to work with this student. Keeping a clear record will demonstrate your commitment and avoid ambiguity.

Whenever you work with a student to solve an academic or behavior issue, it's helpful to keep a record of it. Having a record makes it easier to spot patterns—both in students' behavior and in your own practice. It might not seem like the fourth time you've had to speak to a particular student about off-task talking in class, but when you see your notes add up, you'll realize it's time for a conference or a call home. Similarly, you might have a few lectures that you love to give each year, but if you notice that you're dealing with increasing issues of student disengagement on those days, perhaps it's time to rethink your lesson plans.

Records can also be helpful if a situation continues or escalates and it becomes necessary to involve administrators, counselors, or parents or guardians: they can give background information and context, and they can also communicate the efforts you've already made in relation to this issue.

How you keep these records is up to you—maybe you have a favorite app or an affinity for index cards—but the system you use should be

- easy to access whenever you need it
- customizable
- able to handle a school year's worth of notes
- searchable.

Personally, I find it easiest to keep all of these kinds of notes in a single table—that way, I can add and organize information easily. Figure 5.21 shows an example of notes I wrote after an incident.

As you get into the habit of making these notes, pay attention to how you're feeling as you write them. You might feel a sense of satisfaction when something is resolved in a positive manner. Other situations might result in frustration, anger, or embarrassment; problem-solving can bring conflict, even when we are trying hard to work with students rather than against them. Instead of letting those feelings color your descriptions of the incidents or your perceptions of your students, you may decide to keep

Student Name	Contact Details	Incident Details and Attempts to Resolve
Edlin, Allen	8/22—3:05 p.m. Conferred with Allen 8/22—3:10 p.m. Mother: Julie Sales Cell: 000-000-0000 8/22—4:05 p.m. Counselor: Sally Bight (left message)	**8/22** Left class for washroom at 2:09 just as bell rang. Returned at 2:19. As Allen reentered, I told him his lateness would count as a tardy (gone 10 minutes and washroom is right around corner from classroom). At the end of class, I talked with Allen about the tardy and said I would drop the tardy in return for dialing back his daily washroom pass requests during 3B homeroom and 7th. Allen seemed frustrated/angry (responded, "Whatever . . ."). Said it takes him a long time to use washroom. Talked to mom to see if there were any unresolved medical issues. None that she was aware of, but Mom said she would talk to Allen and possibly take him to the doctor. Thanked me for calling. Left Allen's counselor, Sally, a voicemail to check in, share situation, and see if there's anything else I might be missing—she's been working with him for a couple of years and may have more context.
Summarize what happened—the actions of all involved—keeping the description purely factual. Here, remember: our own perceptions of our students are affected by what we choose to pay attention to. If you find yourself writing very long notes about negative incidents, ask yourself: Will this tight focus on the student's negative behaviors truly help the student change their behaviors for the better? A simple record of the situation might be more helpful overall.		

Figure 5.21 **Notes should be detailed and as objective as possible.**

another set of notes: "How Did This Incident Affect Me?" Tracking your own thoughts and feelings may help you see what "pushes your buttons" and let go of frustration and hurt. Use *I* statements to note how you felt: "I felt angry when Anna rolled her eyes at me," for example. Later, after you've had time to calm down, you can revisit these notes and consider how you might reframe the situation. For example, you might think to yourself, "I took Anna's actions to mean that she didn't respect me, but they might not have been about me at all. Anna has been struggling with the work we've been doing this marking period. Her behavior today might have been an attempt to save face. This is something I can work on in general: if I start to feel as though a student is being disrespectful, I can try to remember that these conflicts are rarely just about me or about a student's feelings about me."

MOVE>Use a Proactive Approach with Supervisors, Deans, Principals, and Guidance Counselors

Immediate Result: You get expert help when you need it.

Long-Term Result: Your supervisors and your students' guidance counselors see you as someone who is eager to learn, to take responsibility, and to put your students first. Your students benefit from the solutions that you work out. If a problem escalates, the administrator already has been appraised of the situation and understands your history in attempting to work out a feasible resolution.

At times, it is necessary to enlist the aid of an administrator or guidance counselor when attempting to solve a problem that you have been unable to resolve alone. Don't feel bad. That's why they're there. It's their job to be attuned to working with parents, guardians, students, and teachers to solve a problem positively in a way that enables the student to become a successful classroom member and learner. Yet, when you're asking these staff members to intervene, it's important to view them as the last resort. Directly involving the dean or assistant principal in a student discipline matter means you've exhausted all other options. And if that is truly the case, these administrators will most likely work with you wholeheartedly to help you resolve the issue. But if you expect administrators to intervene in situations that you might be able to resolve by working with students and their parents or guardians, you may receive a lukewarm reception when you come knocking on their door.

I've seen concerns about being seen as needy or weak keep teachers from reaching out to administrators and guidance counselors, even when they could have used their support. These teachers—particularly teachers who are new to a school and eager to prove themselves—worry that they need to go it alone in order to be considered competent by their administration. They don't want to be seen as a bother or as a weak link. This is a tough road to take. It requires teachers to prioritize order over what's best for individual students. It also keeps those teachers from benefiting from the collective wisdom in their buildings.

Luckily, there's a better way. When you're facing a challenging situation, there's absolutely nothing wrong with knocking on an administrator's door, describing the situation, and asking for their advice. You might say, "If you were in my shoes, how would you solve this problem? What do you think would be the best course of action that will get the student back on track academically as well as eliminate a disruption?" The administrators in charge of student discipline have seen it all, including a lot of actions that didn't solve the problem. They have a lot of insight into student issues that is just waiting to be tapped. Take advantage of this tremendous resource (see Figure 5.22).

Likewise, guidance counselors also have tremendous insight they can share with you since they work with the same group of students over multiple years. When you see a problem, it is smart to touch base with the student's guidance counselor sooner rather than later. It's highly likely they will have some tips for working with that student that will solve the problem a lot faster than if you try to go it entirely on your own.

Figure 5.22 **When you view administrators in the role of advisers and collaborators, not firefighters, even problems that escalate are far more likely to be resolved in ways that serve students, teachers, and parents and guardians.**

How's It Going?

The "honeymoon" is long over. You and your students have settled into the routine of school, which can turn into a long grind to the end of the semester or year or blossom into a series of epiphanies and breakthroughs. The trick is to see problems as opportunities for learning rather than as frustrating, anxiety-producing roadblocks.

The questions that follow pose some potential issues and problems along with the page number of a move that could offer guidance. If you make a check, go back and take a look at that move. If you make several checks, take a breath and decide which problem needs to be solved first. Don't try to tackle everything at once: every solution will require sustained effort from you and your students and, as you've probably noticed in your teaching life, too many initiatives result in too many forgotten, unfulfilled initiatives. To decide what to tackle first, ask yourself: Which of these, when solved, will give my students the greatest happiness, success, and safety in my class?

- ☐ Are your students not at the top of their game after too much Halloween candy, after an extra-long winter break, or because of a bad case of spring fever? (page 166)

- ☐ Do your students have a hard time settling down at the beginning of class? (page 175)

- ☐ Do your students have focusing issues when transitioning from one classroom activity to another? (pages 168, 171, and 175)

- ☐ Are students missing a necessary interaction skill or learning skill that is interfering with their work? (page 171)

- ☐ Is there a classroom problem (forgetting to clean up, voicing complaints in unproductive ways, using phones in inappropriate ways, and so on) that needs to be solved? (page 175)

- ☐ Do you want to improve your kid-watching skills and offer even more positive feedback? (page 181)

- ☐ Are you offering positive feedback to all students in a somewhat equal fashion? (page 181)

- [ ] Would you like to have fun during conference night by encouraging students to lead the discussion of the accomplishments and learning goals? (page 186)

- [ ] Do you have to make a difficult phone call to a student's home? (page 189)

- [ ] Are you feeling frustrated by a student's disappointing behavior decisions? (page 199)

- [ ] Are you dealing with a student-to-student interaction that has resulted in a he said/she said/they said situation? (page 206)

- [ ] Are a student's negative behavior decisions keeping you up at night? Pushing you toward your breaking point? (pages 206 and 208)

- [ ] When you work with students on disappointing behavior, have you kept accurate records? (page 213)

- [ ] If your interventions with a student do not seem to be working, have you turned to administrators for advice well before you may be sending a student to them? (page 216)

If you hardly checked anything off, then this year you will have the opportunity to try some of the more aspirational ideas listed in the Re-energize the Work and Bolster Alliances sections of this chapter. If you've checked off a lot of things, don't feel bad. Some years offer more opportunities for us to problem-solve than others. Just remember to pick one problem and solution to work on at time, and keep this in the back of your mind: Many times solving one classroom problem well ends up solving a slew of problems in the end! While you may not be able to imagine it in the moment, when the conclusion of the semester or school year rolls around, you and your students will genuinely miss one another, a sign that important relationships grew and blossomed over the course of the class.

REFERENCES AND INSPIRATIONS

Ackerman, Courtney. 2017. "Reality Therapy: Constructing Your Future One Choice at a Time." Blog, August 31. https://positivepsychologyprogram.com/reality-therapy/.

Adams, Douglas. 1979. *The Hitchhiker's Guide to the Galaxy*. London, UK: Pan Books.

Ahmed, Sara K. 2018. *Being the Change: Lessons and Strategies to Teach Social Comprehension.* Portsmouth, NH: Heinemann.

Armstrong, Thomas. 2016. *The Power of the Adolescent Brain: Strategies for Teaching Middle and High School.* Alexandria, VA: Association for Supervision and Curriculum Development.

———. 2019. *Mindfulness in the Classroom: Strategies for Promoting Concentration, Compassion, and Calm.* Alexandria, VA: Association for Supervision and Curriculum Development.

Beers, Kylene, and Robert E. Probst. 2017. *Disrupting Thinking: Why How We Read Matters.* New York: Scholastic.

Benson, Jeffrey. 2014. *Hanging In: Strategies for Teaching the Students Who Challenge Us Most.* Alexandria, VA: ASCD.

Braff, Danielle. 2019. "Joe Maddon Meditates, and the Cubs Have a Mental Skills Coach: How the Team Uses Mindfulness and Encourages Kids to Do the Same." *Chicago Tribune*, May 8. www.chicagotribune.com/lifestyles/ct-life-cubs-mindfulness-parenting-0507-story.html.

Braithwaite, John. 1989. *Crime, Shame, and Reintegration*. Cambridge, UK: Cambridge University Press.

Bright, Melissa A., Sarah D. Lynne, Katherine E. Masyn, Marcus R. Waldman, Julia Graber, and Randell Alexander. 2018. "Association of Friday School Report Card Release with Saturday Incidence Rates of Agency-Verified Physical Child Abuse." *JAMA Pediatrics* 173 (2):176–82. https://jamanetwork.com/journals/jamapediatrics/article-abstract/2717779.

Carver-Thomas, Desiree, and Linda Darling-Hammond. 2017. "Teacher Turnover: Why It Matters and What We Can Do About It." Palo Alto, CA: Learning Policy Institute. https://learningpolicyinstitute.org/product/teacher-turnover-report.

Cavazos, Shaina. 2016. "Schools Combine Meditation and Brain Science to Help Combat Discipline Problems." *Chalkbeat*, April 6. www.chalkbeat.org/posts/in/2016/04/06/schools-combine-meditation-and-brain-science-to-help-combat-discipline-problems/.

Confident Counselors. 2017a. "Conversations: Phone Calls from an Angry Parent." *Confident Counselors*, October 27. https://confidentcounselors.com/2017/10/27/phone-calls-angry-parent/.

———. 2017b. "7 Simple Ways to Calm an Angry Parent and Improve Parent Communication." *Confident Counselors*, November 27. https://confidentcounselors.com/2017/11/27/calm -angry-parent/.

Cozolino, Louis. 2013. *The Social Neuroscience of Education: Optimizing Attachment and Learning in the Classroom*. New York: W. W. Norton.

Curwin, Richard L., Allen N. Mendler, and Brian D. Mendler. 2018. *Discipline with Dignity: How to Build Responsibility, Relationships, and Respect in Your Classroom*. 4th ed. Alexandria, VA: Association for Supervision and Curriculum Development.

Daniels, Harvey. 2017. *The Curious Classroom: 10 Structures for Teaching with Student-Directed Inquiry*. Portsmouth, NH: Heinemann.

Daniels, Harvey, and Elaine Daniels. 2013. *The Best-Kept Teaching Secret? How Written Conversations Engage Kids, Activate Learning, and Grow Fluent Writers*. Thousand Oaks, CA: Corwin.

Daniels, Harvey, and Nancy Steineke. 2004. *Mini-Lessons for Literature Circles*. Portsmouth, NH: Heinemann.

———. 2014. *Teaching the Social Skills of Academic Interaction*. Thousand Oaks, CA: Corwin.

David Lynch Foundation. "The Quiet Time Program: Improving Academic Performance and Reducing Stress and Violence." www.davidlynchfoundation.org/schools.html.

Dibinga, Omékongo. 2017. "Elevating the Black Male: Strategies to Become a More Culturally Competent Teacher." February 20. www.upstanderinternational.com/elevating-black-male -strategies-become-culturally-competent-teacher/.

Durlak, Joseph A., Roger P. Weissberg, Allison B. Dymnicki, Rebecca D. Taylor, and Kriston B. Schellinger. 2011. "The Impact of Enhancing Students' Social and Emotional Learning: A Meta-analysis of School-Based Universal Interventions." *Child Development* 82 (1): 405–32.

Elias, Marilyn. 2013. "The School-to-Prison Pipeline." *Teaching Tolerance* 43 (Spring): 38–40. www.tolerance.org/magazine/spring-2013/the-school-to-prison-pipeline.

Emdin, Christopher. 2016. *For White Folks Who Teach in the Hood . . . and the Rest of Y'all Too*. Boston: Beacon Press.

Fay, Jim, and David Funk. 1995. *Teaching with Love and Logic*. Golden, CO: Love and Logic Press.

Ferriter, Bill. 2016. "Simple Truth: Kids Want to Be Noticed." *The Tempered Radical* (blog), July 2. http://blog.williamferriter.com/2016/07/02/simple-truth-kids-want-to-be-noticed.

Finkle, David Lee. 2019. *Mr. Fitz*. Comics from March 11–13, 2019. www.mrfitz.com/strips.php ?date=2019-03-11.

Finnis, Mark. 2018. "33 Ways to Build Better Relationships." *Independent Thinking*, April 6. www.independentthinking.co.uk/blog/posts/2018/april/33-ways-to-build-better -relationships/.

France, Paul Emerich. 2018. "A Healthy Ecosystem for Classroom Management." *Educational Leadership* 76 (1). www.ascd.org/publications/educational-leadership/sept18/vol76/num01 /A-Healthy-Ecosystem-for-Classroom-Management.aspx.

Frey, Nancy, Douglas Fisher, and Dominque Smith. 2019. *All Learning Is Social and Emotional: Helping Students Develop Essential Skills for the Classroom and Beyond.* Alexandria, VA: Association for Supervision and Curriculum Development.

Fry, P. S. 1983. "Process Measures of Problem and Non-problem Children's Classroom Behavior: The Influence of Teacher Behavior Variables." *British Journal of Educational Psychology* 53 (1): 79–88. https://onlinelibrary.wiley.com/doi/abs/10.1111/j.2044-8279.1983.tb02537.x.

Gehlbach, Hunter, and Carly Robinson. 2016. *Creating Birds of a Feather: The Potential of Similarity to Connect Teachers and Students.* Washington, DC: American Enterprise Institute. www.aei.org/wp-content/uploads/2016/08/Creating-Birds-of-a-Feather.pdf.

Glasser, William. 1988. *Choice Theory in the Classroom.* New York: HarperCollins.

———. 1998. *Choice Theory.* New York: HarperCollins.

Glover, Matt, and Ellin Oliver Keene, eds. 2015. *The Teacher You Want to Be: Essays About Children, Learning, and Teaching.* Portsmouth, NH: Heinemann.

Gonzalez, Norma, Luis C. Moll, and Cathy Amanti, eds. 2005. *Funds of Knowledge: Theorizing Practices in Households, Communities, and Classroom.* Mahwah, NJ: Lawrence Erlbaum Associates.

Goudvis, Anne, Stephanie Harvey, and Brad Buhrow. 2019. *Inquiry Illuminated: Researchers Workshop Across the Curriculum.* Portsmouth, NH: Heinemann.

Grizenko, Natalie, Michael Zappitelli, Jean-Philippe Langevin, Sophie Hrychko, Amira El-Messidi, David Kaminester, Nicole Pawliuk, and Marina Ter Stepanian. 2000. "Effectiveness of a Social Skills Training Program Using Self/Other Perspective-Taking: A Nine-Month Follow-Up." *American Journal of Orthopsychiatry* 70 (4): 501–509. https://online library.wiley.com/doi/abs/10.1037/h0087662.

Hammond, Zaretta L. 2014. *Culturally Responsive Teaching and the Brain: Promoting Authentic Engagement and Rigor Among Culturally and Linguistically Diverse Students.* Thousand Oaks, CA: Corwin.

Hattie, John. 2009. *Visible Learning: A Synthesis of Over 800 Meta-analyses Relating to Achievement.* New York: Routledge.

Hertz, Christine, and Kristine Mraz. 2018. *Kids First from Day One: A Teacher's Guide to Today's Classroom.* Portsmouth, NH: Heinemann.

Hillocks, George Jr., and Michael Smith. 1991. "Grammar and Usage." In *Handbook of Research on Teaching the English Language Arts*, edited by James Flood, Julie M. Jensen, Diane Lapp, and James R. Squire, 591–603. New York: Macmillan.

Hopkins, Gary. 2007. "Dealing with Angry Parents." *Education World*, January 22. www.educationworld.com/a_admin/admin/admin474.shtml.

Jago, Carol. 2005. *Papers, Papers, Papers: An English Teacher's Survival Guide.* Portsmouth, NH: Heinemann.

Jang, Nancy. 2010. "Dealing with Angry Parents." *Top Teaching* (blog), November 18. www.scholastic.com/teachers/blog-posts/nancy-jang/dealing-angry-parents/.

Jha, Amishi P., Ekaterina Denkova, Anthony P. Zanesco, J. E. Witkin, J. Rooks, and Scott L. Rogers. 2019. "Does Mindfulness Training Help Working Memory 'Work' Better?" *Current Opinion in Psychology* 28: 273–78. https://miami.pure.elsevier.com/en/publications/does-mindfulness-training-help-working-memory-work-better.

Johns, Beverly Holden. 2015. *15 Positive Behavior Strategies to Increase Academic Success.* Thousand Oaks, CA: Corwin.

———. 2018. *Techniques for Managing Verbally and Physically Aggressive Students.* 4th ed. Austin, TX: Pro-Ed.

Johnson, David W. 2009. *Reaching Out: Interpersonal Effectiveness and Self-Actualization.* 10th ed. Boston: Allyn & Bacon.

Johnson, David W., and Roger T. Johnson. 2018. "What Is Cooperative Learning? An Overview of Cooperative Learning." www.co-operation.org/what-is-cooperative-learning.

Johnson, David W., Roger T. Johnson, and Edythe Johnson Holubec. 2008. *Cooperation in the Classroom.* Revised ed. Minneapolis: Interaction Book Co.

Jung, Lee Ann, and Dominique Smith. 2018. "Tear Down Your Behavior Chart!" *Educational Leadership* 76 (1): 12–18.

Kapp, Diana. 2013. "Raising Children with an Attitude of Gratitude: Research Finds Real Benefits for Kids Who Say 'Thank You.'" *Wall Street Journal*, Dec. 23. www.wsj.com/articles/raising-children-with-an-attitude-of-gratitude-1387839251.

Kohn, Alfie. 2018. *Punished by Rewards.* 25th ed. New York: Houghton Mifflin Harcourt.

Ladson-Billings, Gloria. 2009. *The Dreamkeepers: Successful Teachers of African American Children.* San Francisco: Jossey-Bass.

LaMeres, Clare. 1990. *The Winners Circle: Yes, I Can! Self-Esteem Lessons for the Secondary Classroom.* Newport Beach, CA: LaMeres Lifestyles Unlimited.

Lane, Barry. 2015. *After The End: Teaching and Learning Creative Revision.* 2nd ed. Portsmouth, NH: Heinemann.

Leithwood, Ken, and Pat McAdie. 2007. "Teacher Working Conditions That Matter." *Education Canada* 47 (2): 42–45. www.edcan.ca/wp-content/uploads/EdCan-2007-v47-n2-Leithwood.pdf.

Lieber, Carol Miller. 2009. *Getting Classroom Management Right: Guided Discipline and Personalized Support in Secondary Schools.* Cambridge, MA: Educators for Social Responsibility.

Linsin, Michael. 2011. "How to Handle an Angry Parent." *Smart Classroom Management*, March 26. www.smartclassroommanagement.com/2011/03/26/how-to-handle-an-angry-parent/.

Lipton, Bruce H. 2016. *The Biology of Belief: Unleashing the Power of Consciousness, Matter, and Miracles.* 10th ed. Carlsbad, CA: Hay House.

Making Caring Common Project. 2014. "The Children We Mean to Raise: The Real Messages Adults Are Sending About Values." Harvard Graduate School of Education. https://mcc.gse.harvard.edu/reports/children-mean-raise.

Mathis, Meghan. 2017. "How to Respond to an Angry Message from a Parent." *We Are Teachers*, January 30. www.weareteachers.com/respond-to-an-angry-message/.

McGinnis, Ellen. 2012. *Skillstreaming the Elementary School Child: A Guide for Teaching Prosocial Skills*. 3rd ed. Champaign, IL: Research Press Publishers.

McGregor, Tanny. 2018. *Ink and Ideas: Sketchnotes for Engagement, Comprehension, and Thinking*. Portsmouth, NH: Heinemann.

Medina, John. 2018. *Attack of the Teenage Brain! Understanding and Supporting the Weird and Wonderful Adolescent Learner*. Alexandria, VA: Association for Supervision and Curriculum Development.

Mendler, Brian, Richard L. Curwin, and Allen N. Mendler. 2008. *Strategies for Successful Classroom Management: Helping Students Succeed Without Losing Your Dignity or Sanity*. Thousand Oaks, CA: Corwin.

Miller, Donalyn, with Susan Kelley. 2014. *Reading in the Wild: The Book Whisperer's Keys to Cultivating Lifelong Reading Habits*. San Francisco: Jossey-Bass.

Milner, H. Richard IV, Heather B. Cunningham, Lori Delale-O'Connor, and Erika Gold Kestenberg. 2018. *These Kids Are Out of Control: Why We Must Reimagine "Classroom Management" for Equity*. Thousand Oaks, CA: Corwin.

Minor, Cornelius. 2019. *We Got This. Equity, Access, and the Quest to Be Who Our Students Need Us to Be*. Portsmouth, NH: Heinemann.

Mitchell, Corey. 2016. "Bungling Students' Names: A Slight That Stings." *Education Week* 35 (30): 1, 10–11. www.edweek.org/ew/articles/2016/05/11/mispronouncing-students-names-a-slight-that-can.html?cmp=SOC-SHR-FB&print=1.

Moll, Luis C., Cathy Amanti, Deborah Neff, and Norma Gonzalez. 1992. "Funds of Knowledge for Teaching: Using a Qualitative Approach to Connect Homes and Classrooms." *Theory into Practice* 31 (2): 132–41.

Moore, Eddie Jr., Ali Michael, and Marguerite W. Penick-Parks. 2018. *The Guide for White Women Who Teach Black Boys*. Thousand Oaks, CA: Corwin.

Mraz, Kristine, and Christine Hertz. 2015. *A Mindset for Learning: Teaching the Traits of Joyful, Independent Growth*. Portsmouth, NH: Heinemann.

Muhtaris, Katie, and Kristin Ziemke. 2015. *Amplify! Digital Teaching and Learning in the K–6 Classroom*. Portsmouth, NH: Heinemann.

National Center for Complementary and Integrative Health (NCCIH). 2016. "Meditation: In Depth." https://nccih.nih.gov/health/meditation/overview.htm.

O'Connell, Patrick M. 2017. "Can In-School Meditation Help Curb Youth Violence?" *Chicago Tribune*, January 2. www.chicagotribune.com/news/ct-classroom-meditation-disadvantaged-students-met-20161231-story.html.

"Parent, Family, Community Involvement in Education." 2008. NEA Policy Brief. www.nea.org/assets/docs/PB11_ParentInvolvement08.pdf.

Plevin, Rob. 2016. *Take Control of the Noisy Class: From Chaos to Calm in 15 Seconds*. Bethel, CT: Crown House.

Posey, Allison. 2019. *Engage the Brain: How to Design for Learning That Taps into the Power of Emotion.* Alexandria, VA: Association for Supervision and Curriculum Development.

Ray, Katie Wood, with Lester Laminack. 2001. *The Writing Workshop: Working Through the Hard Parts (and They're All Hard Parts).* Urbana, IL: NCTE.

Rice, Punita Chhabra. 2017. "Pronouncing Students' Names Correctly Should Be a Big Deal." *Education Week*, November 15. www.edweek.org/tm/articles/2017/11/15/pronouncing -students-names-correctly-should-be-a.html?cmp=eml-enl-tu-news1&M=58277832&U =175859&print=1.

Sacks, Ariel. 2017. "Three Tips for Planning the First Day." *Teaching for the Whole Story* (blog), *Education Week*, August 31. http://blogs.edweek.org/teachers/whole_story/2017/08/three _tips_for_planning_the_fi.html.

Schonbrun, Zach. 2020. "Why Home Field Advantage Is Not What It Used to Be." *The New York Times*, Jan. 11. https://www.nytimes.com/2020/01/10/sports/football/road-team-advantage .html.

Schwartz, Patrick. 2006. *From Disability to Possibility: The Power of Inclusive Classrooms.* Portsmouth, NH: Heinemann.

Silver, Debbie, Jack C. Berckemeyer, and Judith Baenen. 2015. *Deliberate Optimism: Reclaiming the Joy in Education.* Thousand Oaks, CA: Corwin.

Steineke, Nancy. 2002. *Reading and Writing Together: Collaborative Literacy in Action.* Portsmouth, NH: Heinemann.

———. 2009. *Assessment Live: 10 Real-Time Ways for Kids to Show What They Know—and Meet the Standards.* Portsmouth, NH: Heinemann.

"Tips and Tricks: Dealing with Angry Parents." 2013. *One-Stop Counseling Shop* (blog), March 21. https://onestopcounselingshop.com/2013/03/21/tips-tricks-dealing-with-angry-parents/.

Toshalis, Eric. 2015. "Five Practices That Provoke Misbehavior." *Educational Leadership* 73 (2): 34–40.

Tovani, Cris. 2004. *Do I Really Have to Teach Reading? Content Comprehension, Grades 6–12.* Portland, ME: Stenhouse.

Vogel, Suzanne, and Lars Schwabe. 2016. "Learning and Memory Under Stress: Implications for the Classroom." *Npj Science of Learning* 1 (article no. 16011, June 29). https://doi.org /10.1038/npjscilearn.2016.11.

Vopat, James. 2009. *Writing Circles: Kids Revolutionize Workshop.* Portsmouth, NH: Heinemann.

"What Is SEL?" n. d. Casel. Accessed September 19, 2019. https://casel.org/what-is-sel/.

"Why Teacher-Student Meditation Should Be in Every School." n.d. Accessed November 13, 2019. www.rootsofaction.com/wp-content/uploads/2016/08/8-reasons-why-teacher-student -mediation-should-be-in-every-school.pdf.

Will, Madeline. 2016. "Study: Class Getting-to-Know-You Exercise Can Help Close Achievement Gaps." *Teaching Now* (blog), *Education Week*, August 5. http://blogs.edweek.org /teachers/teaching_now/2016/08/similarities_teachers_students.html.

Willard, Nancy. 2017. "Teachable Moments on School Bullying: Schools Must Collaborate with Students to Spread Civility." *District Administration*, September 18. https://district administration.com/teachable-moments-on-school-bullying/.

Wood, Chip. 2007. *Yardsticks: Children in the Classroom, Ages 4–14.* 3rd ed. Turners Falls, MA: Northeast Foundation for Children.

Wormeli, Rick. 2007. *Differentiation: From Planning to Practice, Grades 6–12.* Portland, ME: Stenhouse.

Wubbolding, Robert E. n.d. "About Reality Therapy." Accessed November 13, 2019. www .realitytherapywub.com/index.php/choice-theory/.

———. n.d. "WDEP System." Accessed November 13, 2019. http://www.realitytherapywub .com/index.php/wdep-system/.

Zanesco, Anthony P., Ekaterina Denkova, Scott L. Rogers, William K. MacNulty, and Amishi P. Jha. 2018. "Mindfulness Training as Cognitive Training in High-Demand Cohorts: An Initial Study in Elite Military Servicemembers." *Progress in Brain Research* 224: 323–354. https://www.sciencedirect.com/science/article/pii/S0079612318301225?via%3Dihub.

Zemelman, Steven, Patricia Bearden, Yolanda Simmons, and Pete Leki. 1999. *History Comes Home: Family Stories Across the Curriculum.* Portland, ME: Stenhouse.